Tales of the Dancing Rabbit

The Dancing Rabbit Gallery
American Indian Art

Katie McClain Richarme

Michael Richarme, Ph.D.

Cover: Southwest Mountains, original oil painting by J. Barnsley.

ISBN: 1535290390
ISBN-13: 978-1535290395

Copyright © 2016   Katie McClain Richarme and Michael Richarme, Ph.D.

All rights reserved. No part of this work covered by the copyright may be reproduced or distributed in any form or by any means, except as permitted by U.S. copyright law, without the prior permission of the copyright owner.

Library of Congress Catalog Control Number: 2016948333

Printed in the United States of America. Print year 2016.

Forewords

by Ira Wilson, Indian Pueblo Cultural Center - I grew up in border towns on and off my beloved Navajo Reservation. From childhood I was surrounded by Native American Art. I come from family that on both my father's and mother's sides we are strong hearted, artistically inclined and absolutely connected to tradition and mother earth. I was raised with a sense of awareness that not everything is as it seems and if something is too good to be true it probably is. I was taught we are responsible for our people and we must protect and carry on that sacred fire.

As the current manager of Shumakolowa Native Arts inside the Indian Pueblo Cultural Center those values are even more important today. I have 25 years of experience in the world of Native American art. I have seen it change and grow in many exciting ways over the years. I have witnessed it in its booming heyday and through its deepest lows. A time where imitation jewelry and crafts flooded a once healthy market and more notably shady people wanting to turn a fast buck and cash in on Native American culture. What I have learned during these formidable years is that it takes a unique and brave spirit to respect and understand the importance of the true appreciation of traditional Native American art.

Four generations strong, Katie and her family I can proudly say, are keepers of the sacred fire. I knew from the very moment I met her she had the very rare trait of completely understanding that Native American arts and crafts are not things to simply be admired. Inside each vessel there lives history, tradition and masterful skill. Each are extensions of a people that have known real struggle and yet celebrate the blessing of life in every piece created.

I am very humbled and grateful I have found a kindred spirit and sister in arms fighting the good fight. There is a certain love one must have for this particular art form. It is one that has survived incredible odds and continues to grow and blossom into a distinguishable form of fine art. Representing this art form properly is no small task. It literally is an encyclopedia's worth of knowledge and passion that must be condensed into a few phrases for new enthusiast's to grasp the beauty of it. It also must be fiercely protected. It is a wonderful challenge and one we both whole heartedly enjoy. Much respect to Kathy and Michael for putting together this book you are about to read. We have put many miles on our vehicles traveling dusty but beautiful reservation roads and have been in many artist's homes learning and sharing life. Each family we have met is a new adventure and a new story to tell.

by Lyn Fox, Lyn A. Fox Fine Pueblo Pottery – The Dancing Rabbit Gallery has been with us for a while. It was founded in 1980 by Jo McClain; a bricks and mortar expression of a life-long immersed in the love and profound respect for native art and culture. Jo and her husband Pat passed that love and passion on to their daughter Katie who has put her own imprint on the family legacy. Katie is far more than a Native American art dealer, though she is a fine one. Her blogs show a tireless search for an ever deeper understanding of and empathy for the people who are the makers of the timeless objects that she sells; those artists are today's sharers. In a sense, so is Katie.

This generous spirit results in an approach to her business that is far more inclusive than exclusive. There is pottery, jewelry, fetish carvings, weavings, fine art. All pueblos are represented in her inventory as are Maricopa, Hopi, Navajo arts and others. There is old and new; there are recognized stars and Indian Market ribbon winners as well as artists who are just beginning their careers and needing someone to believe in them. All find a home with Katie; all are welcome.

Similarly in her wonderful blogs, there is a warmth and lack of pretense. For example, here from her blog called The Tafoya Ollas, she says this about her encounter with Santa Clara potter Toni Roller:

"...watching Toni hold the pots that her mother and grandmother had made 80 or 90 years ago seeing the glow in her eyes and the smile on her face as she looked back on those fond memories, and hearing her tell the stories about her mother and grandmother --that was the real treasure..."

This is about more than business or money. On her website Katie talks about how her parents wish was to share their gallery with others. This is Katie's legacy and now she shares with us. In a write-up on a piece of pottery by Jemez potter Dominique Toya, Katie says: "She continues to delight and amaze..." The same can be said about Katie Richarme.

Flute Player by Kelly Haney

Woodrow Haney's Flute
(father of Kelly Haney)
Subject of Flute Player painting

Preface

Welcome to *Tales of The Dancing Rabbit*. We hope you have a wonderful time reading our tales of adventures throughout the American Southwest. Our stories are written from our hearts, with a few additional stories contributed by Jamie McClain.

Storytelling is an expression of art, and we have found that the more one knows and understands about the artist, the people, and the culture surrounding the art, the more expressive the storytelling becomes. If one knows the story of Romeo and Juliet, for example, then the opera becomes more than just nice songs.

So our challenge is to bring you some of the art of Native Americans of the American Southwest, and to relate some of the stories behind the art. Our stories will capture some of our adventures in the pueblos, talking to current artists and gaining a better understanding of not only their craft, but also the personalities of the artists. We will also write about artists who have already passed, trying to bring to life some of the stories that they told. Sometimes the information is biographical, and sometimes it is stories that were passed down through our family records.

Almost every morning, we sit in the Gallery or on the back porch, discussing our adventures or recalling poignant childhood memories. The stories are generally written from Katie's perspective, using her words, though Michael listened very carefully, and he did most of the writing. As with all other things, we find this team approach to be quite satisfying.

So come join us on this journey through the world of Native American culture and storytelling. Thank you for your time, and if you have any suggestions or comments, please feel free to email. We would love to hear from you.

Katie McClain Richarme
Michael Richarme
and Tanner, our faithful puppy

Our Tales

	page
It All Began With This Little Black Pot	1
The Matriarchs and Their Lineages	2
Respecting Traditions	4
What's In A Name?	6
The Cycle of Life	8
Storytellers	10
Brave Little Warrior Mouse	11
Michael's Conversation with Navajo Code Talker Chester Nez	12
Seeking Forever Homes	14
Zuni Pueblo	16
A Visit with David Dawangyumptewa, Hopi Artist	17
The Dancing Rabbit Gallery Turns 35 Years Old in 2015!	18
The Beauty of Art	20
Keshi, The Zuni Connection	22
Touring the Jemez Mountain National Scenic Byway	24
A Day with Dominique Toya	26
Trading Posts Then and Today	28
Taos Pueblo's Blue Doors	30
A Visit to Acoma Pueblo - Sky City	31
Artistic Talent Has Many Outlets	32
Toadlena Trading Post	34
Baskets are a Beautiful Addition to Any Collection…	36
Clicks or Bricks?	38
Adobe Gallery and Al Anthony, Jr.	39
A Visit with Kim Seyesnem Obrzut, Hopi Bronze Sculptor	40
Northern Arizona's High Desert and Mountains	42
Northern Arizona – Towns, Museums, and Serendipitous Discoveries	44
Northern Arizona and the Grand Canyon	46
Northern Arizona – Flagstaff and More Artists	48
Zuni Fetishes	50
Southwestern Volcanoes	52
Fall Begins to Emerge	54
Thanksgiving and the Lowden Pot	55
Cluster Work – Magnificence in Native American Jewelry	56
Christmas Stories	57
Nacimiento – Native American Nativity Sets	58
Christmas Celebrations	60
The Story of Farolitos and Luminarias	62
The Southwestern Christmas Tree	63
Resolutions for 2016	64
National Park Service Preserving Traces of the First Americans	66
The Long and Winding Road	68
Chaco Canyon	70

More Tales

	page
The Legacy of Margaret Tafoya	72
The Tafoya Ollas	74
The Agony of the Pot	76
The Ecstasy of the Pot	78
A Visit With Toni Roller	79
Hanging Out at the Heard	80
Territorial Indian Arts & Antiques Gallery	81
Retrospective on the 2016 Indian Market at the Heard Museum	82
What is Heishi and How is it Made?	84
Memories of Past Santa Fe Indian Markets	86
Halona Inn at The Zuni Pueblo	87
The Robert Nichols Gallery	88
IFAM's Second Year	89
Emerging Artists at Indian Market	90
Indian Market Reflections	92
Museums – Curators of Culture	94
Indian Pueblo Cultural Center – A Story of Cooperation	96
A Lucy Lewis Retrospective	98
Starbucks at the Indian Pueblo Cultural Center	100
Laguna Potter Stacey Carr	101
People of Action	102
Water	104
Repair and Restore	106
Rugged and Beautiful	108
Enoch Kelly Haney, Seminole/Creek Statesman and Leader	110
A Simple Piece of Silver	111
Quirky Jerome, Arizona	112
It's Just a Rock … Guest Story by Jamie McClain	113
Joe Hayes and Tortilla Flats… Guest Story by Jamie McClain	114
Biscohitos - A Family Christmas Tradition… Guest Story by Jamie McClain	116
Slumgullion Pass and Historical Markers… Guest Story by Jamie McClain	117
Boredom Becomes Stardom – Briefly… Guest Story by Jamie McClain	118
The Old "58"… Guest Story by Jamie McClain	120
When I Met Charlie Eagleplume… Guest Story by Jamie McClain	121
Window Rock, Arizona – Navajo Nation Home	222
Meeting Samuel Manymules, Navajo Potter Extraordinaire	124
Which Squash Blossom Necklace Would You Choose?	126
A Winters Chill	127
Santa Fe – A Spectacular Place to Explore	128
Standing Bear Powwow	130
Turquoise Inlaid Wood	131
A Walk in the Forest	132

It All Began With This Little Black Pot...

This little pot represents the beginning of a multi-generational appreciation of Native American art and culture - and my family's private collection. This little pot was purchased by my great-grandmother from Maria Martinez in her home at San Ildefonzo Pueblo in 1934 during a family vacation from Oklahoma to Red River, New Mexico. The purchase price was $3.00!

That summer vacation marked the beginning of what would become an annual event - going to New Mexico. The drive across several states always seemed to culminate in the little town of Red River, with numerous stops along the way to experience culture, appreciate the arts, and to purchase souvenirs. Four generations of my family have spent many happy times exploring and learning about the Native Americans of New Mexico—and it all began with a little black pot.

San Ildefonso pot, Maria Martinez, circa 1934.

The Matriarchs and Their Lineages

One of the most exciting aspects of being a gallery owner is the ability to travel the American Southwest to discover new treasures. Some of these treasures come from estate sales, and other treasures are acquired directly from artists. Earlier this week, I was reflecting on some of the adventures that Michael and I have had in the past few years, and it brought me back to some of the memories of my mother. She and my dad did the same thing several decades ago, spending weeks crisscrossing the Southwest and finding exciting pieces of art. As a small girl, I was with them on those journeys, but I didn't realize at the time the significance of what they were doing.

My parents were not big time collectors, or fancy gallery owners. They were very limited in both scope and means, and were very selective in what they did. As part of their travels, they went to the "best of the best," what we know today as the Matriarchs of pottery. During the Anglo expansion into the American Southwest in the early part of the 20th century, Native American art became very collectible, and was rapidly transported back to the Eastern states. Though Native American potters had been making functional pottery for centuries for their daily use, a number of them quickly realized that they could make extra pots for the tourist trade and create a business. As a result, Mother was able to meet and build long-term relationships with many of these potters, including the select few who became recognized as the Matriarchs. And as I go through my own journeys and form my own relationships with Native American artists, I am continually drawn back to recognizing the path on which my parents traveled and how that is so parallel to my own.

A Matriarch is typically defined as the head of a household or tribe. In this sense, Matriarch is used to reflect the best Native American potters of that era, who laid the foundations for a new and highly collectible art form. Many sources recognize a half-dozen or more true Matriarchs, such as Nampeyo of Hano (Hopi), Maria Martinez (San Ildefonso pueblo), Lucy Lewis (Acoma pueblo), Margaret Tafoya (Santa Clara pueblo), Helen Cordero (Cochiti pueblo), Marie Z. Chino (Acoma pueblo), Frog Woman (Zia pueblo), and Paqua Naha (Frog Woman, Hopi). Some might include others in this select grouping, such as Rose Williams (Navajo) or Rose Gonzales (Santa Clara) for the innovations they contributed. Because this is a completely subjective assessment, some might argue for the deletion of certain names from this list or the inclusion of others, which is fine.

One of the amazing aspects of my mother's activities is that she not only met and built relationships with these Matriarch, but she also formed several lifelong friendships with them and their families. Some of these memories are recounted in future stories, and are part of our treasured family history.

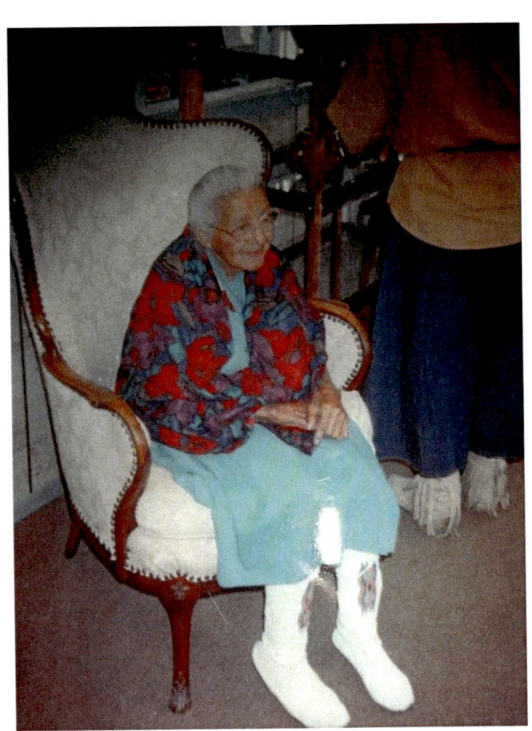

Margaret Tafoya, Matriarch potter, Santa Clara pueblo

Lineages also figure into this story, as the Matriarchs often passed along their skills and talents to their children. Rose Williams, for example, passed along her talent to her daughter Alice Cling, who also passed that along to her own daughter, Michelle Williams. The very talented and prolific potter Margaret Tafoya had many children who became expert potters, and one strand of her lineage runs through her daughter Toni Roller, Toni's sons Cliff and Jeff Roller, and Jeff's sons Ryan and Jordan Roller. In fact, if you rightfully include Margaret Tafoya's mother, Sara Fina Tafoya, one can count Ryan and Jordan Roller as seventh-generation expert potters.

Another lineage that has developed expert potters is that of Maria Martinez (Pond Lily) of Sal Ildefonso pueblo. Individually, and also in conjunction with her husband Julian, she continued a thousand year tradition of pueblo pottery making and extended it into the art world. She recreated both the historic polychrome designs of generations past as well as developing the oxygen-reduction technique that produced today's well-known black-on-black finish. Her niece Carmelita Dunlap came to live with her as a young girl when Carmelita's mother sadly passed away at an early age, and Carmelita learned at the hands of a master potter. Carmelita's daughter, Martha Appleleaf, took up the art, as did Martha's son Erik Fender (Than Tsideh, Sun Bird). Now Erik's son Ian and grandson Talyn are also making pottery, and will be doing so with the expert guidance of their father and grandmother.

As I mentioned, Mother was honored to build friendships with most of the very talented Matriarchs, and even had some like Ivan and Rita Lewis, Juan Tafoya, and others drop by their Santa Fe home to stay for short visits (usually coinciding with Santa Fe Indian Market). Mother and Rita became best friends, and mother was heartbroken as she later attended Rita's funeral.

*Maria Martinez,
Matriarch potter
San Ildefonso pueblo*

I am also honored to carry on the tradition started by my great-grandmother, grandmother, and mother, in getting to know the artists and their culture. It is so wonderful to see my friends when we travel to the American Southwest, to be greeted as a friend, and welcomed into their lives. I have gotten to know a number of artists and their families over the years, and it is so much fun talking to someone like Carmel Lewis about her mother Lucy and my mother Jo. The same is true of the Roller family, the Fender family, and many others where our family roots are intertwined over the generations.

I am fortunate to be able to indulge my passion for Native American art in this way. Learning the stories of the artists, their culture, their backgrounds, and even their families brings much more substance to the art they produce. No longer just a lump of fashioned clay, even with the pretty designs and form, but much more of a peek into the soul of the artist himself or herself. Their art enriches my soul, and the relationships I have formed have enriched my heart as well. That becomes the driving force for my gallery, and why I strive to tell the stories that I tell in the way in which I tell them.

So the next time you have an opportunity, spend a few minutes and talk to an artist. Learn something of who they are and how they feel, and gain some insights into what their art says. From that first encounter, you will embark on a wonderful, rewarding journey and will never look at a piece of art quite the same way again.

Respecting Traditions

Every culture on this planet has its own traditions. After all, that is what helps to establish and continue a culture – the ways in which we do things. Understanding the traditions of a culture can give us a lot of insight into what the culture values, and also gives common ground for discourse and trade.

Some cultures have religious traditions, such as the Christian celebration of Christmas, the Jewish celebration of Hanukkah, and the Islamic celebration of Ramadan. Other celebrations are more secular and prosaic, such as the fairly ubiquitous celebrations held by many countries of the anniversary of their founding or independence.

Interweaved among these traditions are instructions, handed down from generation to generation, carefully honed by centuries of experience, that help us navigate through life. We've often heard the joke that babies come without users manuals, but in reality they do. In days gone by, villages raised children, and everyone was involved in making sure that rules were learned and sanctions for bad behavior were clearly understood. I knew, when I was a small child, that if I did something wrong at a neighbor's house, I would be scolded by that mom, and she would tell my mom so I would be scolded again when I got home. That network of everyone helping everyone seemed to work fairly well. At least it did for me.

So we grow up knowing one culture and one way of doing things. Exposure to different cultures can be somewhat jarring, as they may do things in different ways. Our natural responses, when faced with something different, are to reject it as somehow bad, to try to change it to what we already know, or to learn from the differences and understand that different cultures can coexist in harmony.

Unfortunately, the history of the Anglo hasn't been particularly understanding. As European settlers spread from the East coast toward the West, many of them brought with them a conversion doctrine. "My way is right," they said, "so you should change your traditions to look like mine." This doctrine led to unbelievable levels of suffering and outright disaster for the Native Americans.

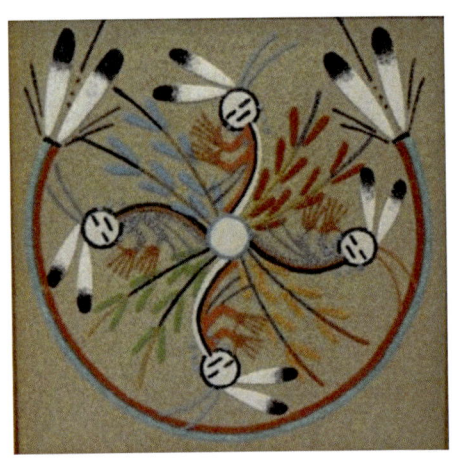

Whirling Wind Log sand painting, J.B. Josk, Navajo, circa 1989.

Today, I hope and pray that we are learning from these past tragedies. Different does not mean better or worse than my perspective, it just means different. We can learn so much from different cultures, different ways of doing things, and different perspectives on how we live in this world. The more that we learn, the less that we fear, and the more suited we are to take good pieces from each culture to enrich our own lives.

My many friends of different cultures know that I have an almost insatiable appetite to learn about their cultures. I know that there are certain boundaries that cannot be crossed, and I completely respect those who politely tell me that certain areas are off-limits. I think my friends know that I am not being nosy just to be nosy, but I am asking questions because I really want to know and understand, as best I can, their lives and their perspectives.

Each culture adds different strands of color to the rich tapestry that is humanity. When we have a chance to step back and look at the overall composition, it is simply stunning in its complexity and richness. The languages, the songs, the arts – they all give voice to this vibrant story. I write these tales to tell my part of the story, but also to try to shine some lights on the many varied traditions of the Native Americans of the Southwest.

Swaying Man Ngayayataqa Katsina, Hopi Pueblo, circa late 1940s.

Zuni Olla Maiden Dancers, Heard Museum, circa 2015.

What's In a Name?

I have often been asked how I came up with the name *The Dancing Rabbit* for my gallery. Honestly, I didn't. My mom and dad started The Dancing Rabbit Gallery back in 1980, at the time primarily concentrating on Oklahoma painters like Jerome Tiger, Kelly Haney, Archie Blackowl, Gary Montgomery and others. They collected and sold the works of these artists and many others.

When I was a child, my family would always take a summer vacation to New Mexico, Arizona, and Colorado. Southwestern history, art and culture figured in my life from very early on.

So I thought in selecting a name for their art gallery, my parents must have given it very careful consideration. My father, a fiery red-headed aerospace engineer, traced his family lineage back to the kilt-wearing Lochbuie clan in far western Scotland. His family emigrated from Scotland in the 1800's and finally settled in Oklahoma. My mother, a warm-hearted educator, taught children's classes at Fort Worth's Museum of Natural History. Her family had emigrated from England in the 1800's as well, and eventually called Oklahoma home. When my parents retired and got a second home in Santa Fe, my mother was asked to consult at the Wheelwright Museum, because of her extensive Native American artifact background. Surely, I thought, with them both growing up immersed in Native American cultures and building wonderful relationships with Native American friends, they carefully chose the *Dancing Rabbit* name and logo to reflect some aspect of their interest in Native American culture.

The original logo for The Dancing Rabbit Gallery, 1980.

Sadly, both of my parents passed away during the 1990's, and they aren't here now to answer all of the questions I have for them. I have scrutinized all of the family photos, letters, and other documents, and have asked my younger siblings for any information that they might have. Slowly, a picture has emerged of their lives, and of their parents and grandparents as well. It is amazing how we don't think to ask these questions, or make observations about our families when we are kids growing up, or even when we are young adults raising our own families. Only later in life, when we have time to reflect, do these things become increasingly important.

How wise it is of the Native American peoples to capture their traditions in oral stories, and pass along those stories to their children early and often in life. With my tales, I hope to capture some of the stories that they tell with their lives and with their art, always respectful of the private areas they don't wish to be disclosed. I also hope to capture some of the adventure and wonder that Michael and I are enjoying with our travels through the American Southwest, meeting and getting to know new people and building wonderful relationships with them. I've been asked many times about the *Dancing Rabbit* name, and always responded that it was a mystery to me, but must have had important significance.

The good news is that my mother's younger sister spent some time with us over this past Christmas, and I posed many questions to her. One that she was able to answer was the start of the Dancing Rabbit name. It turns out that my father's father settled in McAlester, Oklahoma, and stayed there until he went off to college. My mother's parents moved back to McAlester (where my maternal grandfather also went to high school) when my mom was a teenager, and she finished her high school years at McAlester High School, where she met another McAlester high school student-- my dad. Nature took its course, they both went off to college together, got married, and started a family.

Later, when they decided to open their gallery, they went back to the time when they first met, and chose the gallery name from the mascot of their high school – the Dancing Rabbit! McAlester has subsequently opened a new High School, and adopted the Buffalo as their mascot, retiring the Dancing Rabbit to posterity. All of those years that I have had my maternal grandfather's high school yearbook from 1918 with the Dancing Rabbit mascot on the cover, and I never made the connection until my dear, sweet aunt answered my question. One mystery solved - many more yet to go.

Emma Lewis, sister of Lucy Lewis, Acoma pueblo, circa 1990s.

A story told is a story to remember.
A story lived is a story to be retold.

The Cycle of Life

Mother Earth continues to spin in her orbit about the sun, and the seasons change with predictable regularity. Much of our lives fall into familiar patterns, and we sometimes find ourselves unconsciously repeating the steps taken by our parents and grandparents. This recently came home to me in a very emotional way.

It was a typical Monday morning, and Michael and I had just completed our morning coffee and were off to our respective tasks. For Michael, Monday mornings generally mean grading student assignments, so he grudgingly ambled off to his office. I began what I enjoy the most – learning new things about Native American culture, artists, and their works.

To a large degree, I learn things from three major sources. The first source is the Internet, and we all know that everything on the Internet is true, right? But sometimes this source does give me a decent starting point, particularly if I am just starting to scratch the surface of an area.

The second source I consult is my network of experts – artists, gallery owners, and those who have a lot of information in the specific area of my interest. I love to have conversations with folks who have pieces of knowledge, and are so generous with their time and information to help me feed my almost insatiable appetite for knowledge.

The third source is one that I use extensively. My own reference library has well over a hundred books, not including the fictional ones that are often founded in the lore of the Southwest. Some of these books are just printed, and yes, I do confess a certain addiction to getting an author-signed copy of a reference book. Something about that connection just makes me tingle a bit.

But many of the reference books I have are either those I purchased years ago, or those which were initially acquired by my mother or grandmother in their research activities.

Tohono O'odham Papago Figural Basket, circa 1940s.

Earlier, I was looking in a Papago basketry book, as I had just acquired a beautiful large figural basket, most likely from the 1940's or 50's, and I wanted to do some more research on the techniques the Papago used to make their baskets. I knew a bit about their basketry methods, but wanted to check several of my reference books to make sure.

Imagine my surprise when I opened the book and found a Santa Fe New Mexican newspaper page from the 1994 Indian Market, listing the winners by category. Immediately, I knew the source of the page – that was the very last Indian Market and very last trip my mother took to her beloved New Mexico before she passed away a few months later. She tucked this page away in the reference book (likely because of the size of the book pages, rather than the subject), probably suspecting that I might come across it one day. Thirty-one years later, almost to the anniversary of her passing, I opened the book and found her treasure for me.

Reference Book with Santa Fe New Mexican newspaper article, circa 1994.

My emotions swirled about for the remainder of the day. Yes, I do miss my mother, and wish that she could be here to see how I have tried to honor her legacy with The Dancing Rabbit Gallery. But in addition to honoring the foundation that she laid for me, I have also tried to build upon that foundation with my own efforts.

I read some of the names of the 1994 Indian Market Winners, names like Jeff Roller and Nancy Youngblood, preeminent Santa Clara potters. I feel like I am continuing my mission of learning the stories of these artists and sharing them with the world, highlighting their talents and skills, faithfully and respectfully portraying their vibrant cultures and varied backgrounds.

The cycle of life continues. Older artists teach the young, and then the young rise to their places of prominence. Skills and techniques are passed down, and the young (as often is the case) expand the scope of the art. As humans, we are fragile and only around for a limited number of years. But knowledge can be transferred from cycle to cycle, from person to person, from artist to artist. The fundamental traditions and culture of Native Americans are built on this premise. Listen to the stories, and pass along your knowledge to the young ones. That is the greatest gift we can give them.

Storytellers

For Native Americans, traditions are passed from one generation to the next through the telling of stories. Though the words may occasionally change, there is always a main theme, key points to convey to the young ones, and conclusions about how one should live one's life. The telling of stories, or passing along an oral history of tradition, is highly respected among the Native American peoples, and is visible in all aspects of their lives.

The time honored Indian pueblo pottery tradition of working with clay and telling stories has merged into a modern art form of 'storyteller' pottery dolls. The art of making clay effigies is as ancient as the Anasazi peoples who inhabited the deserts of New Mexico many centuries ago. During the latter portion of the twentieth century, it was the Cochiti pueblo potters who were known for clay effigies depicting many different aspects of their everyday life. Yet, it was not until 1964, that Helen Cordero of the Cochiti pueblo created her first 'storyteller' figure. I love the tradition of passing down stories of family culture and history to the next generation. The image of small children gathered around a grandmother or grandfather to hear accounts and adventures of long ago lingers with me from my own childhood memories of listening to my great-grandmother share her adventures in Indian Territory (later known as Oklahoma).

Modern storyteller dolls were originally created by Cochiti artist Helen Cordero in 1964, although other potters like Laurencita Herrera were already creating "singing mothers." Originally, Helen created open mouthed female figures with children in their arms and called these dolls "Singing Mothers." She eventually made a male figure, modeled after her grandfather, Santiago Quintana, with children clinging to his back and in his lap, playing the drum and singing songs of the stories of their heritage and traditions. Cordero believed a male

Various Storytellers (l-r) Buffy Cordero, Laurencita Herrera, Rita and Ivan Lewis, Maxine Toya.

doll was more appropriate, as males were traditionally the storytellers in her tribe. They quickly gained in popularity and many other artists in Cochiti started making them as well. As time went on, more and more artists started making their own storyteller dolls, each adapting their own unique style and implementing their own beliefs based on their heritage. In the Gallery I have several made by close personal friends of my parents, Ivan and Rita Lewis, as well as one made by Helen Cordero's granddaughter Buffy Cordero Suina.

Today, the term storyteller refers to any human or animal figure that is covered with smaller children or animals. They have become one of the most collectible and sought after forms of clay art. It is estimated that there are well over 200 Pueblo potters now creating storytellers. Every potter has their own special clay, technique, tools, and colors that are used to create their art. Most artists collect their own clay from the earth, and still use the traditional firing techniques that take place in the ground. Among the most notable families making storytellers today are the Fraguas of Jemez Pueblo and the Tellers of Isleta Pueblo. The mud heads of Dorothy and Paul Gutierrez and the owls of Zuni are but different forms of storytellers- the ones who pass on the culture and traditions of the people.

Adapted from *Pueblo Stories and Storytellers* Mark Bahti and other sources

Brave Little Warrior Mouse

One of my favorite katsinam (plural for the Hopi word katsina, often shown as kachina by Anglos) is the little Hopi Warrior Mouse. While not actually a katsina, he has earned himself a respectable place in the hearts of young and old alike for being courageous and daring. I acquired this Warrior Mouse at the Heard Museum in Phoenix in 2000, and a delightful young clerk told me the rest of the story.

As the story goes, the village was being threatened by a nasty old hawk - he was eating all the village chickens. The old men knew he must be killed, the boys knew he must be killed, and all the women and children knew he must be killed - but no one knew how, and all their efforts had failed. The Village Chief and Town Crier were very worried and had met in private to smoke and ponder upon the subject. Even they did not know how to rid themselves of the marauding hawk. Then late one night, a little mouse sat smoking in his little kiva - and he felt bad for the people and decided that he would kill the hawk. So that night he went to the home of the Village Chief.

He told the Village Chief he was going to kill the hawk. Although the Town Crier and the rest of the village shook their heads in disbelief, some thought maybe the mouse had special power, so they prepared anyway. A date was set, and preparations took place. The mouse had sharpened the end of a greasewood stick and dug a long tunnel from his kiva into the plaza. There he dug another hole reaching to the surface. The hawk sat watching from far away. He was angry with this mouse and flew off to destroy him - but the mouse danced close to the opening of his kiva and ducked inside each time the hawk came close.

Then finally he went into the tunnel he had dug and drove the sharp spear up through the ground next to the opening in the earth, and he went back out singing and dancing. Only this time he went far away from his kiva, and all the people thought the hawk would get him for sure. It was just then that the hawk swooped down low to snatch up the pesky mouse, but the mouse dropped down into the hole he had dug, and the hawk, who did not see the spear in the ground, impaled himself.

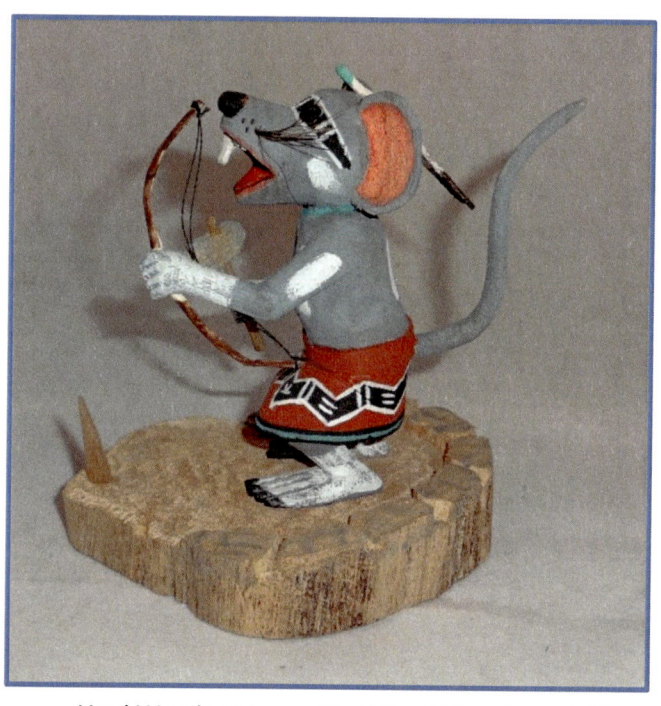

Hopi Warrior Mouse, Neal David Sr., circa 2000.

The villagers were amazed, and the little mouse was honored as a hero - and they celebrated. And that is how the mouse defeated the hawk.

The Hopi and the Navajo often use the katsinam as teaching tools for their young. Their stories are parables that pass along to young Native Americans the traditions and values of the pueblo or tribe. Each katsina has a story, and is far more than just the lovely wood carving. So the next time you see a wonderful katsina, ask about the story – it will be time well spent.

Michael's Conversation with Navajo Code Talker Chester Nez

During World War II, the United States was locked in a bitter struggle with the Japanese Empire on islands throughout the South Pacific. The Marines recruited a group of 29 Navajo (Dine) men to create a code language for artillery direction, and then to implement the language on the very dangerous front lines facing fanatical Japanese soldiers. A number of books and even Hollywood movies have been created about this group, called the Code Talkers.

One year ago, my wife and I went to Albuquerque for the first weekend of the Balloon Fiesta and to visit some of our gallery friends in Albuquerque. While there, we stopped at the Indian Pueblo Cultural Center to see some of their exhibits and visit their gift shop manager, Ira Wilson. Of course, Katie couldn't resist getting a nice Ganado Red rug and a lovely Michael King necklace.

But the highlight of the trip for me was quite a surprise. There was a poster outside the gift shop that Chester Nez, the last living member of that original group of Code Talkers, would be signing copies of his new book, appropriately titled *Code Talkers*, that afternoon. We had a couple of hours to wait, so we went into the adjoining restaurant where my anticipation built and built.

Finally, it was time. I got my book from Ira, and took it over to Chester at his table. At 93, Chester was frail but still had a knowing gleam in his eye. I asked him to please sign my book, and he did so. Then, I used the only word of Navajo that I know, Ahééhee', three times.

The first time, I said Ahééhee' for his service during the War, saving countless thousands of American lives with his courage and dedication.

Chester Nez, Navajo Code Talker.

The second time, I said Ahééhee' for his being such a wonderful role model to young Navajo men who can struggle with the challenges presented by reservation life.

The third time, I said Ahééhee' for being a personal inspiration to me. As a young boy, I read volumes on the Second World War, as did most young boys of my generation. The values that I took from those volumes included honor, hard work, trust, teamwork, courage, perseverance, and many others. Though he didn't know it at the time, Chester Nez and his generation sacrificed to give me liberty and freedom. They formed my character, though sometimes that formation took extra work to round off some of my stubborn rough edges.

I carried his book home with me, and to this day it remains on my nightstand, one of my treasured possessions. It is much more than just a book to me; it is a daily inspiration.

Eight months after I had my brief talk with Chester, I learned that he had passed away at the age of 93. I sat in my office, read his obituary, said some quiet prayers for Chester and his family, and shed some tears. I am so blessed that Katie and I just happened to be in Albuquerque that first weekend in October, and that Chester was signing books. This year, as the Balloon Fiesta draws near, Chester won't physically be there. But I have his book, signed by his hand, and I have the treasured memories of a very brief conversation with Chester. His spirit will always be with me, and I will try very hard to pass along his inspiration to my children and grandchildren. For that is how we grow as humans, seeing the best in people and trying to include those aspects in our own lives.

So, Chester Nez, once again I say Ahééhee' for being the man you were. Yes, the one word I know in Navajo means thank you.

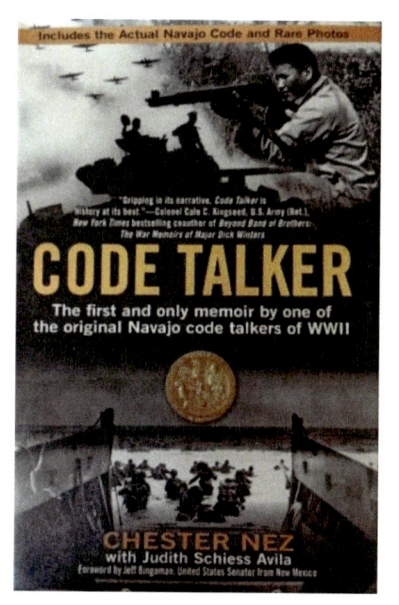

Code Talker book by Chester Nez, Navajo.

Your legacy is determined by the number of lives you touch and by the impact you have on those lives.

Seeking Forever Homes

When I purchase works of art for my Gallery, I always look for those works which have an emotional connection to me. I bring them home, find room for them on the shelves or walls of the Gallery, and sit and admire them each morning. In almost all cases, I simply fall in love with the pieces, knowing the artists (or about the artists) and the meticulous and painstaking effort they put into each piece.

And thus the dilemma appears. If I was merely a collector of fine art, I would be able to love these pieces for the rest of time, ensuring that they travel to a reputable Museum when I pass on. However, Gallery owners don't have that luxury. We are simply the intermediaries between the artists and the forever homes of the art. We purchase works of art from the artists, supporting their endeavors, and provide awareness of the works of art to a wide audience, hoping that someone will similarly be enthralled with an item and bring it into their home.

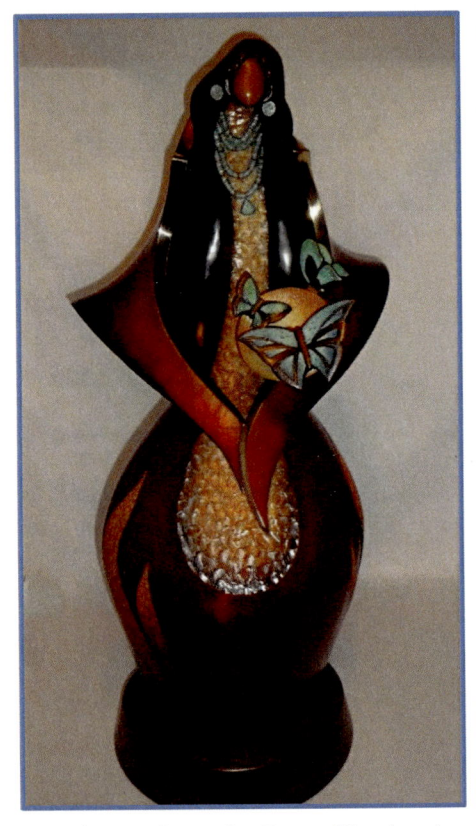

A Place Where the Butterflies Land, Kim Seyesnem Obrzut, circa 2014.

For the collector, it is a new, exciting member of their family. For the Gallery owner, it is a very bittersweet parting, one which I do not particularly enjoy. This was very difficult for me recently, when I sold a signed, limited edition print by one of my favorite Hopi artists, David Dawangyumptewa. I had purchased the print from David at an art show in 1988, when my mother and I were wandering about.

Something about his art – the colors, the motion, and the vibrancy of the figures – really caught my eye, and I immediately brought it home. For the past 27 years, it has been with me every day, when I start the day with the first cup of coffee. That is the second work by this artist I have sold this month.

Often, the artists also have this bittersweet moment when they sell one of their works of art. One and a half years ago, Michael and I were walking through a large artist fair in the city where we live, and we saw a booth set up by a Hopi bronze sculptor, Kim Seyesnem Obrzut.

One of her bronzes, *A Place Where the Butterflies Land*, immediately touched my heart. Michael steered me over to a nearby park bench, where we sat and admired her work for an hour or so. But that one piece kept calling out to me. So, of course, I talked with Kim and her daughter Crystal, and arranged to purchase the piece

This year, when Kim returned to our art show, I purchased a much smaller piece, *The Spirit of Creation*, but still a very beautiful and evocative one.

I also saw a new, large piece she had just finished, *The Matriarch*. I told Kim that I would purchase *The Matriarch* if I could find a forever home for *The Place Where the Butterflies Land*, and she was astonished that I would part with the Butterflies, given that I was almost in tears when I saw it for the first time in the prior year. But I said, yes, as a Gallery owner, I have to be able to give my pieces an opportunity to go to forever homes, even if it is a painful parting.

Having said that, *The Matriarch* never left my mind. Later in the fall, we were in Prescott at the Phippen Museum art show, knowing that Kim would be exhibiting at that show. I made a beeline for her tent, and without any hesitation, purchased The Matriarch.

Fortunately, Kim ships her items, as this one weighs in at about 70 pounds and is about 3 feet tall. So now I have three beautiful pieces by Kim, and I love all of my children, but I know some day one or more will go away to forever homes. And it will be bittersweet.

I've talked about this with other Gallery owners, people I respect like Al Anthony, Lyn Fox, Robert Nichols, and Mark Sublette. They each tell the same story. Gallery owners are in this business because they love the art and the artists, and their souls are enriched greatly by being able to support the artists and to temporarily be caretakers of their art. As one of my friends said recently, "It certainly isn't for the money, as most Gallery owners are quite far from rich."

The love of the art, and the wonderful relationships I am building with the artists, are very rewarding. The art tells a story, and we just have to listen carefully to hear what it conveys. And when an artist passes on, their stories and their legacies remain. Gallery owners are custodians and caretakers of the art and the stories, seeking just the right forever home for the works of art. But it is such a bittersweet profession.

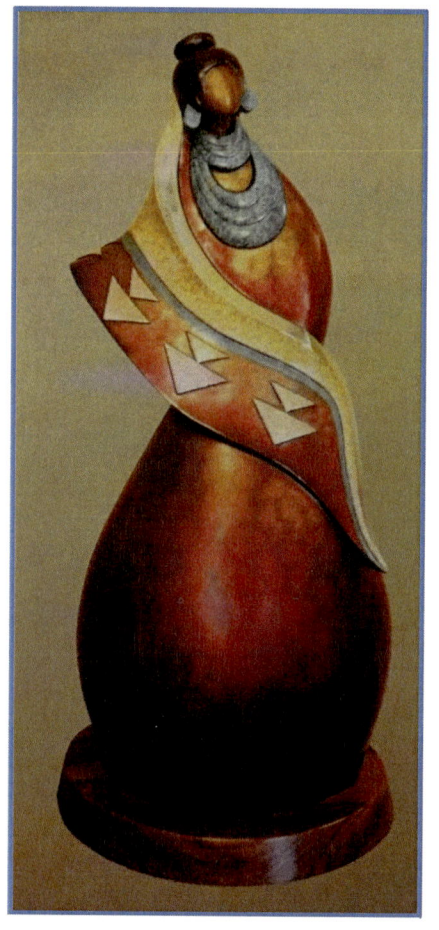

The Matriarch, Kim Seyesnem Obrzut, Hopi bronze sculptor, circa 2015.

Zuni Pueblo

The Zuni pueblo is located in southwest New Mexico, about an hour south of Gallup. Residents here claim (along with the Taos pueblo) to be the longest inhabited pueblo. I won't get into that discussion; let's just say that both pueblos have been continuously inhabited for about 10 centuries and let it go at that.

When you get to Zuni, stop at the Visitor Center and register. They have a nice exhibit of Zuni artifacts, and have a number of informative brochures. That is also where you sign up for the Zuni pueblo tour, a guided tour of the pueblo and Zuni Mission.

Our tour guide took us into the Zuni Mission, and we had a chance to see the incredible murals painted on both inside side walls. The murals are of Zuni dancers representing different aspects of the Zuni culture. It is also an interesting juxtaposition of the Zuni culture and the Spanish Catholic culture in the mission.

Many of the Zuni and Acoma pueblo members have returned to their ancient religious beliefs, unlike many of the other pueblos which still retain the Spanish Catholic faith and traditions.

Zuni Pueblo main entrance, circa 2014.

The Pueblo held their Main Street Festival in May, and just finished the Cultural Arts Expo last week (August 8-10, 2014). Many beautiful pieces of jewelry, lovely fetishes and gorgeous pottery were available for viewing and purchasing. I was not able to be there this year—but I will be next year!

A Visit with David Dawangyumptewa, Hopi Artist

David Dawangyumptewa, Hopi artist. That is what his business card says. But there is so much more to the story of this gracious and highly talented man.

The three mesas of the Hopi Reservation are surrounded by the Navajo Nation, so David grew up with the peaceful, philosophical teachings of the gentle Hopi people, but he also experienced the Navajo in his schooling. As a very young man, David had the typical interests in music and art that all teenagers have, but he took it one step further and learned the difficult skills of stage lighting, enabling him to begin a career as a lighting specialist with a number of rock bands. Some were extended gigs, such as his tour with Linda Ronstadt that began in Miami and ended on the West Coast a number of months later. Others were regional gigs, including artists like Sting. David won a number of awards for his skill at concert lighting, which was just an early indication of his eye for light and perspective.

David moved into painting as his life on the road slowed down, and began interpreting many of the images and stories that he grew up with on the three mesas of Hopi. David's acrylics are bold and vivid, featuring the colors typically associated with the Hopi peoples and his Water clan.

Katie with David Dawangyumptewa, Hopi.

An inner strength carried David through a stroke a few years ago, and he has taught himself to paint with his left hand. The detail and vibrancy of his work continues to leap from the canvas, and it is simply incredible that he continues not only to paint, but to extend his art into mixed media expressions.

I bought a print from David about 20 years ago, and it hangs in my Gallery where I can see it every morning when I have coffee. For years, I have planned to acquire an original from him, and last year when he announced his two-man show at the Museum of Northern Arizona in Flagstaff, I told David that I was coming and ready to acquire one of his originals. We met David for coffee at a wonderful little coffee shop in Flagstaff, went to the Museum to see his exhibition, and then went through the extended agony of figuring out which of his wonderful works spoke to me the most clearly.

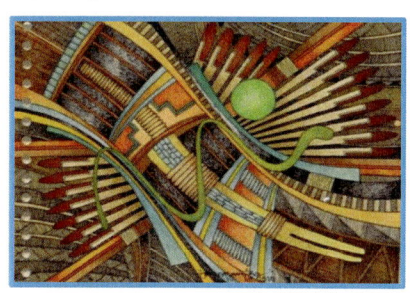

Medicine Bundle, David Dawangyumptewa, circa 2010.

To make a long story short, I picked Medicine Bundle, which is also the one that Michael picked as his favorite. I also was able to get a mixed media artist's proof of another painting, which would be used for producing prints. Even better, David agreed to have dinner with us that evening, so we went to a nice restaurant in Flagstaff and had a couple of hours of great conversation with this highly talented artist.

And that, I suppose, is how I will always think of David – his talent is a gift, but his wonderful personality is what I think of as pure Hopi – gentle, warm, proud of his heritage yet very humble about himself, and very much in tune with Mother Earth. This is the way of Hopi, and David is an amazing, resilient, and wonderful Ambassador to the world of his people and their traditions and lifestyles.

The Dancing Rabbit Gallery turns 35 years old in 2015! Happy Birthday, Dancing Rabbit!

Started in 1980 by my mom, Jo McClain, and my dad, Pat McClain, the Dancing Rabbit Gallery was initially a vehicle by which my parents could indulge their lifelong love of Southwestern American Indian art. Mom was a great fan of Oklahoma painters, including Jerome Tiger (we currently have about 17 of his signed, limited edition prints), Doc Tate Nevaquaya, Archie Blackowl, and Kelly Haney, among many others. She began buying prints, and a few originals when she could afford them, and she and Dad went to a few shows to sell some of the prints. Thus began the official "business" part of the Dancing Rabbit Gallery.

But the story actually goes back more than a century before that. Mom's paternal grandmother, Nellie Hammer Denham, was one of the first Anglo women into the Oklahoma Territory, where she was a schoolteacher for Native American children. When she was a child, Mom's parents would take her on vacation trips to New Mexico, Arizona, Utah, Colorado, and throughout the Southwest, visiting pueblos, learning history, and meeting lots of people. One of the first pieces of pottery acquired by my Mom's mother was a small black pot bought in 1934 from a young lady named Maria Martinez, on the patio of the Santa Fe Governor's Mansion.

Over the years, Mom grew to love the Southwest cultures, and passed that along to me and my siblings when we were young. We too took frequent vacation trips to the Southwest, and Mom and Dad made a point of stopping in to see their many artist friends. It was at that time, on one of our trips, that I began acquiring small pieces of jewelry and pottery (again, as my very limited allowance permitted).

Mom had a part-time job while we were in school, working at the Fort Worth Museum of History in their Native American art and artifacts collection. Personally, I think she would have paid them to work there, as she was completely engaged in her avocation.

Jamie, Maggie, and Katie McClain, circa 1960.

One of the things she did was teach pre-school children about the Native American cultures, and I think this education gene was passed along to me as well. When the Museum decided to downsize their collection, Mom was able to purchase some nice pre-historic artifacts with complete confidence in their provenance.

As time went on, the kids (my siblings and I) moved on to college and our own adult lives, and Mom and Dad became more fully engaged in the Gallery. Though still an aerospace engineer at Lockheed, Dad found time to support Mom with her "habit." They even purchased a small garden home in Santa Fe, where they would spend long vacations visiting with their friends.

Jo McClain at Charlie Eagleplume, circa 1960.

Mom used to tell the story about hearing a knock on her Santa Fe door one day, about a week before Indian Market was to begin. It was Ivan and Rita Lewis, renowned potters, who showed up to visit and stay for a couple of weeks, unannounced. Of course, my Mom took it in stride, and gladly welcomed them into her tiny home for the duration of Market. She told similar stories of Juan Tafoya and other potters who would drop by to visit, and her eyes always sparkled at those fond memories. One of the most poignant stories is of her attending Rita's funeral, and seeing one of Rita's favorite pots smashed into the grave as tradition dictated.

Mom passed away in 1995, and at her funeral, Dad took her favorite Feather Woman pot and did the same. We knew what that meant to Mom, and why she wanted to continue with the traditions she had come to love so much.

Sadly, Dad passed away a few years later, and their collection of art, pottery, baskets, rugs, jewelry, and other artifacts was passed along to my siblings and me. For a number of years, I continued my career as a high school English literature teacher, maintaining my love of Southwestern cultures through visits to the Southwest and a few additions to my part of the inherited collection. But in 2012, as I began to contemplate retirement, a new door opened in my life. My soulmate, Michael, suggested that retirement would give me time to resurrect the Dancing Rabbit Gallery and carry on the tradition that my family began so many years ago. The Internet made that possible, so we re-opened and greatly expanded The Dancing Rabbit to what you see today.

The tradition of education runs strong in my family. My great-grandmother over 100 years ago, in Oklahoma Territory. My grandmother and mother, education young people about the many rich cultures of the Southwestern American Indians. My own career, as a teacher of young minds. There is a common thread, and the pattern that the thread constructs is consistent through the generations.

Pat McClain, circa 1970.

So on July 1, 2015, the Dancing Rabbit Gallery officially turns 35 years old. The tradition and legacy that I continue to represent is well over 100 years old. As the potters and weavers do, I hope to pass along my knowledge and collections to the next generations, so that they too may develop a strong understanding and appreciation for Southwestern Native American cultures and peoples.

In order to know who we are,
    we must know from where we come.
In order to know where we are going,
    we must know who we are.

The Beauty of Art

Beauty is in the eye of the beholder. That is why objective measures of art are so difficult, and so meaningless. Beauty is what speaks to you, deep in your soul. This is what draws me to certain art, and styles of certain artists, more than others. While I grew up with Native American art from the Southwest, my husband grew up with classical French and Italian art. Both are elegant in their own way, but the Native American art calls to my soul as does Michael's preferences calling to his.

So how do we go about gathering those beautiful pieces of art to us? Some people select a theme or color, such as those who collect "cowboy art." Others look to specific media, like pottery, paintings, bronzes, or other media. Some gather art from specific artists, as their preference falls in the style of those artists. Others may just gather pretty things, art that makes them happy.

There is no proper way to go about this process. We all have the freedom to gather art as our taste and budget dictates. As a gallery owner, I have tried to use several themes in building my collections. These may work for you, and they may not. No worries – do what makes you happiest.

My first theme is to look for art that speaks to me. Not necessarily that which will be more readily sold, but that which I am happy to look at each day in my gallery. Art that touches my soul is my first preference.

Following this theme, I look to specific artists whose work I adore. Painters like David Dawangyumptewa, bronze sculptors like Kim Obrzut, stone carvers like Jeff Shetima, potters like Dominique Toya, Erik Fender, Samuel Manymules, and Anderson Peynetsa, silversmiths like Tommy Singer and Kee Yazzie Jr., and many others, all fall in this category. Their works are the most precious in my collections, and in my humble opinion represent the highest and best examples of Native American art from the Southwest. I will be featuring some of these collections in upcoming stories, and sincerely hope that some of what I feature

The Dancing Rabbit Gallery, one wall of pottery.

will stir an interest in each of you about Native American art and the fantastic artists we are fortunate to have among our Native American family.

Another theme is one of family lineages. My mother and grandmother started me down this path, not only collecting but forming life-long relationships with some of the matriarch potters in the New Mexico pueblos. Potters like Maria Martinez, Ivan and Rita Lewis, and Margaret Tafoya were among their friends, and were recognized over time as some of the leading potters in the American Southwest.

It has been my pleasure to follow up with that start, building relationships and collecting pottery from families like the Rollers, who learned at the feet of their maternal grandmother and great-grandmother, Margaret Tafoya. Over the coming months, I will also try to feature some of these lineages in upcoming stories, as the skills and talent seems to transfer from generation to generation, and the traditions are continued and artistry improved.

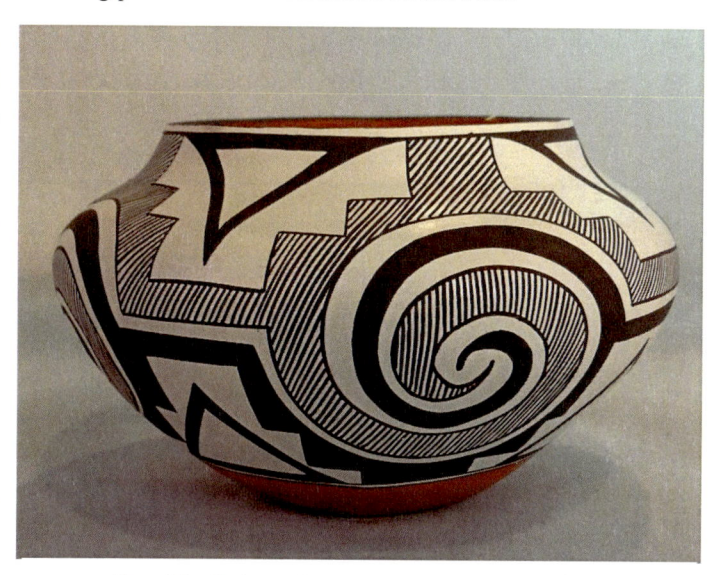

Franklin Peters, Acoma master potter, circa 2015.

And finally, one theme that comes back to me again and again is that of the stories that each piece of art contains. The photography of Debbie Lujan, evoking the thousand-year-old Taos pueblo and its continuing history; the pottery of Bobby Silas and Tim Edaakie, bringing back the traditional patterns of ancient Hopi and Zuni potters; the fetishes of Kateri Sanchez, showcasing corn maidens and owls in her striking work – all these Native American artists have stories of hard work and success behind each of their works of art, and knowing these stories brings their art to life much more for me.

Yes, beauty is truly in the eye of the beholder. I hope to bring you more stories and more pictures highlighting the art that I find beautiful, and continue to celebrate the amazing artists and art found in our own American Southwest among the Native American communities.

Harmony with Mother Earth

Is simply being in tune with the cycles of nature.

Keshi, The Zuni Connection

Keshi (kay-SHE) is the traditional greeting of the Zuni Pueblo people who live in western New Mexico.

The story of the Zuni pueblo continues to fascinate me, and I seem to learn more about this ancient pueblo and its people every day. Recently, on our last trip to Santa Fe, we had the chance to stop in and visit the wonderful people at Keshi, also known as The Zuni Connection.

This retail store was founded in 1981 by Robin Dunlap, and is now run by her daughter Bronwyn Fox-Bern. Initially it was an artist coop established to help the artists of Zuni pueblo with their craft, and it expanded significantly during the Native American art craze of the 1980's and 90's. Through the strong efforts of Bronwyn, the artistic futures of Zuni pueblo and Keshi are happily linked.

The peoples of Zuni formed a series of small villages over a thousand years ago, the largest of which was a pueblo named Halona. Through many centuries of existence in the southwestern New Mexico region, the Zuni peoples formed ties with the Hopi peoples to their northwest, on the Hopi mesas. Trade developed between the peoples, and also the ability to help each other with famines, drought, or other major challenges to their lives.

One of the two big changes to the Zuni peoples came in the 1500's with the arrival of Spanish explorers and missionaries. The peaceful Zuni were overwhelmed with change, sometimes even resulting in the Zuni hiding on nearby mesas until the Spanish left. Occasionally the hiding went on for several years at a time.

Katie outside Keshi, Santa Fe, circa 2015.

But eventually the Spanish took over the Zuni culture, even changing the name of the Halona pueblo to the current name of Zuni pueblo and renaming the people as the Zuni people. The Spanish domination of the Native American peoples lasted until the historic Pueblo Revolt of 1680, when the Native Americans regained their freedom in a bloody uprising.

A second big change to the Zuni peoples came with the western expansion of the United States. The land of the Zuni peoples became a Federal reservation, Anglo traders moved into the area, and the Zuni peoples now had to deal with a different type of domination. The spread of railroads in the latter half of the 1800's opened New Mexico to trade and tourism, leading to entrepreneurs like Fred Harvey who encouraged Native Americans to produce and sell pottery, textiles, jewelry, and other authentic items to Anglo tourists.

For the Zuni pueblo, possibly fortunately or possibly unfortunately depending on your perspective, the main railroad ran about 60 miles north, through the new town of Gallup. That meant Zuni artists, producing fabulous pots, jewelry, and fetishes, had to carry their works to Gallup for sale. So the Zuni pueblo and its people, for the most part, lapsed into a quiet, very basic lifestyle similar to those lived by a thousand years of ancestors in the same location.

The wonderful story of Robin and her daughter Bronwyn, working with Zuni artists and providing a Santa Fe outlet for their works, is heartwarming. The artists are so talented, and yet so few people travel down New Mexico Highway 53 (the Ancient Way) to get to Zuni. Therefore, much of the world doesn't get to know the outstanding works of carvers like Jeff Shetima, Kateri Quandelacy Sanchez, Sandra Quandelacy, and Dee Edaakie, or potters like Anderson Peynetsa, Alan E. Lasiloo, and the team of Tim Edaakie and Bobby Silas, or jewelers like Angie and Wayne Cheama and Effie Calavasa.

Keshi has over 600 different Zuni artists represented in their store. Stop by and get to know the wonderful people at Keshi and learn the stories behind the different animal fetishes, jewelry, and pottery, as well as the different artists who create these beautiful works of art.

Elah-kwa (thank you in Zuni).

Bronwyn and Katie at Keshi, The Zuni Connection.

Touring the Jemez Mountain National Scenic Byway

Roughly 120 miles of highway comprise some of New Mexico's most scenic areas. They are designated the Jemez Mountain National Scenic Byway, and Michael and I had a recent opportunity to explore and take lots of pictures.

We left from Albuquerque on a sunny Friday morning, driving up to San Ysidro for our first stop. This is the only remaining village of the seven original "Pueblos de los Jemez" formed by the Spanish when they entered the area in the late 16th century.

The Jemez people migrated from the four corners region several hundred years earlier, and formed a thriving and peaceful series of pueblos. The Jemez nation had roughly 30,000 people when the Spanish arrived, but fighting and European diseases steadily reduced the population to about 3,000, where it remains today.

On the north end of the Jemez Pueblo is the Walatowa Visitor Center, which has a very nicely done museum (and gift shop) where one can learn much more about the Jemez peoples.

As one travels north along NM 4, the stark red rocks dominate the skyline. There are even car pull-out areas for photographers or just admirers of nature.

When you arrive at Jemez Springs, the Jemez State Monument is also well worth a stop. Run by the US Park Service, you can find the ruins of an ancient Jemez pueblo known as Giusewa and the remains of a 17th century Spanish mission named San Jose de Los Jemez. The short self-guided walking tour brings you right into a reconstructed kiva and the excavated remains of the expansive pueblo. You can also see the impressive mission. The indoor museum has some really nice historic pieces, some excavated from the site and others purposely made to demonstrate the skills of the Jemez peoples.

Slightly up the road, you will drive past the Soda Dam. The hot springs have deposited travertine over the centuries, and water pressure forced a hole into the travertine blockage, creating a most impressive sight from the highway. But take a few minutes, park nearby, and walk up to the top of the Soda Dam and maybe even take off your shoes and dip your toes into the warm water.

Beyond Soda Dam is Battleship Rock, which is a very large rock formation that has the appearance of the prow of a battleship. It dominates the skyline as one approaches from the south, and is framed by the 6,000 foot altitude clear skies and pine and aspen trees.

Soda Dam, Jemez Highway.

When we got to La Cueva, we took a right turn on NM 4 and headed toward Los Alamos. As we headed down the highway, we entered the Valles Caldera, the remains of New Mexico's ancient and very dormant super-volcano. The caldera is a large meadow that stretches to the north, with lots of elk and other critters roaming in this protected land. The Valles Caldera National Preserve has a Visitor Center open from May to early October (we just missed it) and you can even make reservations for elk-viewing tours.

We continued to Bandelier National Monument, which I hadn't visited since I was a small girl. Bandelier is known for 13th century cliff dwellings, and the US Parks Service has done a remarkable job of preservation. Be prepared for the free shuttle bus from the parking area to the park, as there is no significant amount of parking at Bandelier National Monument.

A self-guided walking tour leads you through the cliff dwellings, and people are encouraged to climb around and see how the Native Americans lived eight centuries ago. Bandelier is up in a very peaceful and scenic valley, and it is easy to sit on one of the benches and imagine how the peoples would sleep in the protected cliff dwellings, and then spend their days down on the valley floor engaging in farming, fishing, and other daily activities.

Finally, we departed Bandelier National Monument and headed toward White Rock, the eastern end of the Jemez Mountain National Scenic Byway and the start of our return trip to Rio Rancho. There is a nice little visitor center in White Rock, and it serves nicely as an entry point if you are starting the byway journey from White Rock rather than San Ysidro. The White Rock Overlook has some stunning views of the Rio Grande valley, which has the New Mexico portion of the Rio Grande flowing through it as it makes its way to Texas and then to the Gulf of Mexico.

Bandelier National Monument, cave dwellings circa 1200-1300 A.D.

There are so many things to see and places to visit on this small stretch of New Mexico highway that we weren't able to get to all of them on our short exploration. But now that we have a taste of what is there, we will definitely be back for more. After White Rock, we drove to Pojoaque, down to Santa Fe, and back toward Albuquerque for our long, exciting day of adventure.

A Day with Dominique Toya

It is one thing to know how the Native Americans gather their clay, process it, form and smooth amazing shapes, paint, and then fire the pottery. It is quite another to attempt to create a piece of pottery from scratch. As I recently learned first-hand, it is an extremely time-intensive and laborious process.

Lyn Fox of Lyn Fox Fine Arts in Santa Fe is a well-respected gallery owner, and he has a broad range of historic and contemporary Native American pots in his gallery. He often hosts artist gatherings and workshops, but earlier this month he arranged for something completely different. The event was spending a day at the Jemez Pueblo with one of the most renowned contemporary Native American potters around, Dominique Toya. So, of course, I rapidly registered myself (and Michael) for this day of pottery.

There are a string of pueblos heading north out of Albuquerque and Rio Rancho, including the Santa Ana pueblo, the Zia pueblo, and the Jemez pueblo. We had not been to the Jemez pueblo previously, so we didn't really know what to expect. It was a quick and picturesque drive from our hotel to the Jemez pueblo on a brisk Saturday morning, heading up NM 550 and NM 4. The pueblos are framed by the Jemez Mountains, and the vivid red rock is offset by the volcanic remains of the Valles Caldera (New Mexico's large volcanic crater) and tectonic uplifting revealing many ancient rock strata.

Katie with Lyn A. Fox.

Dominique Toya with Katie, Jemez Pueblo, circa 2015.

We arrived at the Jemez Post Office to be guided back into the pueblo itself. We had a small caravan going through the pueblo streets, arriving at the far back of the pueblo near the Jemez River at Dominique's home. The back of the house has a spectacular view of the Canon de San Diego, rising majestically to the north and west. Going into the house, we were warmly greeted by Dominique's mother, Maxine Toya, also a well-known potter and painter. With typical Native American grace, she welcomed us and gave us some tasty snacks and coffee. Then the fun really began.

Dominique talked to us about how they go into the hills nearby and dig the clay out of the earth. After they bring it back home, they have to clean out all the rocks, roots, and other things that don't belong, ending up with a very pure clay. This is dried and screened into a fine powder, with additional inspections to make sure all impurities are removed. The powder is slowly mixed with water until a moist ball is formed, with continual kneading just like making bread. Fortunately, Dominique had already dug out the clay and cleaned it for us, so after "making the clay," we were each able to begin making a pot.

At each step of the way, Dominique described and demonstrated what to do. We were doing a hand-coil with smoothing after, and this really takes some skill and time. It is a far more elaborate process than the simple pottery wheel and kiln that I use at home, but then again, Dominique's pottery is orders of magnitude better than mine as well. Dominique then showed us how to use our carving tools on the pots, and she demonstrated her amazing swirl that she does by hand, without any measurement other than her eyes.

Finally, our pots were finished, so we set them aside to dry. Knowing that it would take a couple of days to dry before they could be painted and fired, Dominique had already planned for us to complete those last couple of steps. She had prepared Christmas ornament disks that we could paint and fire after lunch, and when our first pots were dry enough, she would fire them and send them to us.

But before we got started on the painting, we had a Jemez feast. Nancy Youngblood (another incredible potter) had stopped by to help, as had Jason Ebelacher (an up-and-coming potter also related to the family). My little head was swirling with excitement, as we had not only one, but FOUR wonderful potters sitting and chatting with us as we had traditional foods including posole (prepared in a big pot outside), enchiladas, red chili sauce with meat, and some amazing biscochitos for dessert. Poor Michael said that he needed a nap after lunch. Nancy graciously headed to the kitchen to spearhead the dish washing, while the rest of us gathered to learn to paint - pueblo style.

So we started painting our ornaments with red-clay slip and white-clay slip. Then Dominique brought out the differentiator – her micaceous slip that gives the pots such a sparkle. While we were painting, she was polishing a small seed pot that would later be finished, and she said that it often takes many hours to polish the pot to give it the sparkle and shine after firing.

We took our ornaments outside, and helped Dominque build a traditional pottery firing – a metal box surrounded by cedar logs, which created an internal temperature of roughly 1200 degrees during the firing. One of the sad aspects of this method is that often a piece that had taken many, many hours to make and paint would crack during the firing, and Nancy showed us an incredible black four-corners vase motif that she had just fired with a single crack at the rim ruining the piece. We had the traditional white-corn meal blessing for the firing, then started the fire.

When the ornaments were done, we let them cool and then took proud possession of our meager efforts. Everyone departed tired and happy, following a most enjoyable day with Dominique, several other Native American potters, and a group of new friends, who learned how to make pots the traditional way, and to gain a greater appreciation of the enormous effort that goes into making a beautiful piece of Native American pottery.

Outdoor pottery firing, Dominique Toya with Katie and friends, Jemez Pueblo, circa 2015.

Trading Posts Then and Today

The first trading posts began on the East Coast, where Native Americans and adventurous Europeans would bring their furs and beaded textiles to trade with European merchants, who would ship the items back to Europe in exchange for items the Native Americans might need, like metal knives, mirrors, or other similar trade goods.

As the Europeans (the new Americans) pushed further west, the Native Americans were either killed through battle or disease, or forcibly relocated to restrictive reservation lands. Many of these reservation lands were either small vestiges of the traditional lands where the Native American peoples roamed, or they were marginally fertile lands for crops or hunting.

That led to the next iteration of the trading post, more commonly seen in the American Southwest. These trading posts were almost like grocery stores, where Native Americans could bring whatever trade goods they could make and acquire basic food items and tools. In many cases, the Native Americans had no concept of the value of their trade goods, so they were at the mercy of either good-hearted or unscrupulous merchants.

Over time, two distinct types of trading posts evolved. The first, the very traditional trading post, oriented around serving the tribe or pueblo in which or near which it was located. Halona Trading Post is a good example, started in the 1890's by Andrew Vander Wagen and still sitting in the center of the Zuni Pueblo and serving the peoples of Zuni. Another outstanding example is the Toadlena Trading Post in the Navajo Nation, where Mark and Linda Winter work diligently to provide the basic necessities of life for their neighbors, while taking in Navajo rugs for resale from the weavers. Mark and Linda purchased the trading post from another owner about nineteen years ago, and reestablished the trading post as a credible and reputable service to their community.

Teec Nos Pos (T'iis Nasbas or Cottonwoods in a Circle) is in northeastern Arizona near the Four Corners Monument. Teec Nos Pos is one of the 110 chapters that comprise the Navajo Nation. Michael and I had a chance to visit recently, and we thoroughly enjoyed our time in the rug room, as well as looking at their lovely pottery and jewelry.

Until this visit, I didn't have a weaving from Teec Nos Pos, but now I do. It is absolutely stunning. The regional pattern that bears the area name goes

Katie at Teec Nos Pos Trading Post, 2015.

back to 1905 when Hambleton Noel came into the area and convinced the residents that he would be just the person to serve the community in the role of trader. Noel was the first white man who was able to win the approval of the local Navajo to set up a trading post on their land. Ten years earlier, two potential traders were driven off. Hamp Noel married Eva Foutz in 1911 and eventually the Foutz family took over the post and still operate it today.[1]

The second type of trading post is a more tourist-oriented retail operation, focusing more on serving tourists than locals. Some are just as old as the traditional type describe above, but tend to spend their efforts on selling trade goods (art works) to tourists rather than food and basic necessities to the local residents. A couple of them that are done extremely well, and that we enjoy visiting, are Garland's Navajo Rugs in Sedona and Than Povi Trading Post at the San Ildefonso pueblo.

As the name would imply, Garland's has a large assortment of large, authentic Navajo rugs sourced from the different chapters of the Navajo Nation – Two Grey Hills, Wide Ruins, Ganado, Chinle, and many others. They have a small but very nice assortment of pottery, kachinas, and jewelry and it is really fun to hang around and chat with them.

Than Povi is a bit different, in that it sits on the San Ildefonso pueblo and is run by Deborah and Elmer Torres, a couple of San Ildefonso natives. Their trading post has been lovingly restored and has the look and feel of a high quality museum or gallery. They have a wide assortment of authentic Native American works of art from many New Mexico pueblos, as well as some great Navajo and Hopi items. The pricing is very reasonable, and if you don't have the time to visit the different pueblos and really don't want to run the risk of buying fake stuff in a retail store, this is a great place to go. As they move more online in the next couple of years, we expect this trading post to blossom nicely.

Garland's Trading Post, Sedona, AZ.

So, at the end of the day, what is a trading post? It is a term that had a lot of meaning a few hundred years ago, and still had some meaning in the Southwest in the middle of the last century. But today, when we think of the term trading post, it really depends on their focus – local residents or tourists. And, as with all retail establishments, there are all levels of quality. Some have great assortments, great pricing, and great service. Others, not so much.

1. Citation from Cameron Trading Post, Cameron, AZ.

Taos Pueblo's Blue Doors

As a young girl, I would visit the Taos Pueblo with my parents and siblings. Back then, the pueblo had very specific areas where tourists could go. I remember walking through the streets and wondering how people lived in the very thick-walled pueblo dwellings, particularly those on the upper levels. And I remember looking at the light blue painted doors and door frames, and wondering if the color had a special significance or meaning.

Today, the Taos Pueblo has a very nice visitor center, and has expanded the areas where tourists can roam. The portion of the pueblo that is still off-limits is clearly indicated, but many of the homes have developed small businesses in the front rooms for expanding their economy. Different families have everything from photography to jewelry to pottery, and then some. Some families have small dining areas for a cool beverage or sandwich, and an opportunity to sit and chat with the residents for a while.

My husband and I have been to Taos a few times in the past couple of years, and we had an opportunity to chat with some really wonderful people as we wandered about the pueblo. One of the questions at the top of my list was to get a better understanding of the blue doors. This came up as I saw a few doors that were painted different colors, not the turquoise blue that I had remembered. Yes, most of the painted doors were still blue, but there were reds, purples, and other colors that startled me a bit. So, of course, I asked. And the answer was quite revealing – there isn't any real significance to the turquoise blue color, other than that it is a very pretty color that is harmonious with the area. No particular significance, no spiritual meaning, no ancient tradition.

Yet the turquoise blue doors of the Taos Pueblo will always be with me. We got some wonderful photographs by Debbie Lujan of the pueblo with the blue doors prominently shown. Though the blue doors may not have significance to anyone else, they will always bring back those great memories of childhood trips to the Taos Pueblo, and will always transport me to the peaceful harmony with nature that the Taos Pueblo and its residents enjoy.

Taos Pueblo, circa 2014.

A Visit to Acoma Pueblo - Sky City

Acoma Pueblo is also known as Sky City. And it is just that - a pueblo located atop a very tall mesa; historically, the pueblo was easily defended, because there were only a few secretive paths up to the top. Once on top of the mesa, the view in all directions is breathtaking. Michael and I enjoyed wonderful a visit to the pueblo this past summer.

When we arrived at Acoma, the first thing we did was to stop at the new Visitor Center at the bottom of the mesa. It has a glorious exhibit of Acoma pottery and paintings, as well as educational films - and a very nice gift shop.

The Visitor Center is where we registered for the Acoma pueblo tour, and shortly after we did so, we had the opportunity to climb in the little bus and head up to the top. It is so much easier than the 370 or so stairs (cut into the living stone) that I had to endure as a little girl and young adult those many decades ago. The first road was a dirt road, constructed in the 1940's for a Hollywood movie; that road was improved and paved in the 1970's for another Hollywood movie. Even better, the Hollywood movie producers not only paid for the roadwork, but also used a number of Acoma residents in the movies!

Living conditions can be harsh on Acoma - water must be carried to the top of the mesa, though the practical Acoma residents have large catch cisterns for rain. There is no electricity on the mesa, so residents use either traditional means or propane gas for their limited power needs. Although there are only a few dozen people who live on the mesa year round, they consider it quite an honor to continue to live as their ancestors did.

Acoma Pueblo, circa 2014.

Acoma Pot, Marie Z. Chino, early 1960s.

As we walked on the tour, we visited with several of the local residents and vendors atop the mesa and made several new friends. The people of Acoma make the most beautiful white-slipped pottery from clay that is gathered around the mesa. I find it most interesting that shards from old pots are ground with the clay to form new pots and it is this combining of the old with the new that provides the clay that is uniquely from Acoma. Artists are known for the very thin walled pots they make.

We thoroughly enjoyed our time at Sky City and have plans to return soon to make more new friends. Through the years I have been fortunate to collect a number of beautiful pieces from Acoma, many of which are currently in the Gallery.

Artistic Talent Has Many Outlets

As the owner of an art gallery, I have the opportunity to do what I cherish the most – mix and mingle with very talented artists and learn their stories. Once I learn about the artist, and maybe even the stories behind individual pieces of their art, each piece takes on much more of a life of its own, and speaks directly to my soul.

I am not sure what drives artistry, or why some people seem to have a "gift" for artistic expression while others can't quite seem to get there. But I do know that this "gift" is rare, and it can be developed and expanded through many years of painstaking practice.

Another thing that I have discovered is that some artists are blessed with multiple ways of expressing this "gift." My friend Debbie Lujan, an amazing nature photographer from Taos Pueblo, has also developed her skill at being a classical violinist, and often plays with symphonies. Another friend, Jeff Shetima of Zuni Pueblo, is one of today's premier fetish carvers, and his eye for composition and motion has led him into nature photography and sketching. Yet another friend, Erik Fender of San Ildefonzo Pueblo, comes from a long line of expert potters, and he is a highly acclaimed potter in his own right, yet he is also moving into sand-cast silver-smithing.

Taos Pueblo photographs, artist Debbie Lujan, circa 2015.

The thing that strikes me about each of these artists is that the skills from one media are not easily transferrable to another. It isn't like driving a Ford, and then being easily able to drive a Chevy. A better analogy might be moving from scuba diving to mountain climbing. Different equipment, different techniques, and different knowledge bases.

Science has shown us that artistic talent often develops in the right side of the brain, which is responsible for spatial orientation, music, and other intangible areas. This is the dominant side of the brain for left-handed people, and as my husband Michael and I are both left-handed, we think about this often. Michael is spatially oriented, and has no troubles with maps or directions, picturing a journey in his mind before beginning. I, on the other hand, try to throw pots on a wheel, expressing my artistic side in that manner. But both of us have a deep appreciation for music and nature, so the opportunity to continue the Dancing Rabbit Gallery, meeting artists and journeying to the beauty of the Southwest, is very fulfilling to both of us.

We've often heard that it takes 10,000 hours of practice to become good at something. I agree with that assessment to a degree. However, I might add that artistic talent is innate in some people, and when they find the appropriate outlet, practice merely enhances the artistry that flows from their soul into their artistic work.

I think that many of the most outstanding artists in the world, in any media, are those who allow their souls to speak to the rest of us. They have a way of communicating directly to our five senses that makes an immediate connection to our own souls. So for me, at least, it is easy to recognize a talented artist or a good piece of art. Does it speak to me, does it connect to my soul?

Knowing the art and the many, many hours of painstaking effort required to create it (particularly with traditional Southwestern Native American art) fires my imagination. Knowing more about the artists, getting to know them and their families on a personal level, deepens my appreciation for their unique talents. And when I happen across an artist who expresses his or her talent in multiple media, I am in awe of both their skills and their willingness to step outside their comfort zone and try new media.

So the next time you gently pick up a piece of Native American pottery, feel around the inside of the pot and touch the smoothed coils. Feel the potter's fingertips as he or she put just the right surface or shine in the pot, and think about how the potter had to gather the clay from the hills, clean the clay, make the coils, patiently build the pot, smooth and paint the pot, and then fire it to hardness.

Do the same with textiles. Think of shearing the wool from the sheep, spinning the yarn, then patiently building the rug and its complicated pattern over many, many hours on the loom.

Katie with Debbie Lujan, Taos Pueblo

Do the same with each piece of art you see, hear, feel, taste, or smell. Think about the toil and labor of the artist to bring that piece of art to life, and how much of the soul of the artist is in the piece. These artists give us each a gift – a window into their souls – and in doing so bring joy and beauty into our own lives.

Toadlena Trading Post

The Navajo Nation covers a huge territory of over 27,000 square miles in Arizona, New Mexico, and Utah. Remnants of the old trading culture still linger, such as Hubbell's Trading Post in Ganado, AZ and Toadlena Trading Post just outside of Newcomb, NM. Outposts such as these were set up for the convenience of the people who live in the area – not for tourists who must find a way to drive beyond the end of the road and around the next corner. If one is adventurous and patient, the drive is well worth it!

I had the opportunity to stop by the Toadlena Trading Post recently, and spent a couple of hours marveling over the assortment of Navajo rugs that they had in the store, as well as wandering through the museum area. Two Grey Hills, Ganado, Chinle, Wide Ruins, and many other parts of the Navajo Nation were well represented, with many weavings from master weavers.

Mark Winter is the owner of the Toadlena Trading Post, and my only disappointment that day was that he wasn't there. As he is the author of one of the seminal works on Navajo textiles, it would have been really nice to chat with him for a bit. However, Thelma filled in nicely with her expert opinions and handy reference materials. I have several rugs, some going back to the 1930's and 1940's, and I was on a quest to learn more about them, as well as a few others for which I had little information.

While I was there, I couldn't resist the opportunity to get another Two Grey Hills rug, partly because of the beautiful patterns and partly because of the very tight weave which makes these rugs so strong and light.

Toadlena Trading Post, Navajo Nation, circa 2014.

At the same time, I got a copy of Mark's newest reference book, and Thelma put it aside to have Mark sign it for me before she shipped it to me. A few weeks later, I received my signed book in the mail.

The next year, we went back to Toadlena, and I finally got a chance to meet Mark and his lovely wife, Linda, and they graciously spent some time with Michael and me talking about the history and philosophy of Toadlena Trading Post. We found the Winters to be warm, friendly, and scrupulously honest, both with their weavers and with buyers. They have managed to transform Toadlena Trading Post into the beating heart of the Two Grey Hills weaver community.

Inside Toadlena Trading Post, circa 2014.

Katie with Mark and Linda Winter at Toadlena Trading Post, circa 2015.

Baskets are a beautiful addition to any collection as well as amazing works of art—and I love them

Basketry is one of the oldest means of carrying and storing foods and materials, like grains or shells. Ceremonial and religious occasions, like weddings, also featured the use of baskets. Made from naturally degradable materials, baskets tend to fade and decompose over time, so it is really hard to get an accurate estimate of when basketry began. Many estimates, using basket impressions on fired pottery, make a case for basketry being widely used as long as 10,000 years ago.

It is something that we have all done as children in summer camps, and it is still widely practiced and utilized around the world today. Baskets available on the market today were probably constructed no more than 120 years ago. Baskets for retail sales became quite popular after the arrival of the railroad in the Southwest. Baskets made between the 1880s and 1950s tend to be the most valuable, particularly if they are in good condition, well-made, and have an interesting design. But these factors can also make a newer basket very desirable.

Many Native Americans have used different materials for their basket weaving, creating ornate and stunning designs. Typically, they used the materials available to them in their local areas, such as the use of yucca, willow, and sumac in the American Southwest. Weavers from different areas developed unique forms and structures in their basketry. Some tribes, such as the Cherokee, developed extremely complicated weaving styles like the double-weave, where an inner wall and outer wall are woven together for strength and durability. Navajo tuss baskets were coated in pinion pitch to make them water tight for storage of water and other liquids.

Most of the American Southwest tribes use the coiled method with local grasses or the plaiting method with wider stems and leaves. Coil baskets are easily recognizable by their spiral coil design, where a starting point at the bottom of the basket is created, and the coil is systematically spiraled around that starting point, stitched together at frequent intervals. Sometimes the stitches are animal sinew, but more often they are composed of other grasses or even threads. This method offers more strength and more opportunity for decoration. We see this

Akimel O'odham geometric bowl, circa 1920s.

technique from the Tohono O'Odham (Papago) baskets, when they created lovely baskets from strips of yucca and Devil's Claw. Navajo (Dine') baskets are commonly made from the sumac and are known for the central knot used to begin the coiling process.

As with many of the Native American art media, the basketry symbols tell stories, like the man in the maze of the Tohono O'Odham. Many other tribes and pueblos used woven symbols, which can be both exciting and challenging to interpret. These symbols are enhanced with colors, with specific materials like yucca giving a green color, Devil's claw creating a lovely black/brown color, or dried or dyed materials providing different colors.

Sometimes it can be difficult to identify baskets from different areas of the world, as many baskets from Mexico or parts of Africa are strikingly similar to those of the Native American basket makers. Even within a specific tribe, basket makers may use slightly different techniques. Unlike pottery, silver jewelry, or paintings, baskets are not signed and thus provenance is challenging to determine. It is imperative when purchasing an authentic Native American basket, you choose a reputable gallery/store which follows the Indian Arts and Crafts Act of 1990, which is "a truth-in-advertising law that prohibits misrepresentation in marketing of Indian arts and crafts products within the United States." (US Dept. of the Interior Public Law 101-644).

Various Native American Baskets and Reference Books.

When you look to the past, you learn from your mistakes.
When you look to the future, you learn from your opportunities.

Clicks or Bricks?

My view of a gallery is that it should be an intermediary between the artist and the art-lover. Each piece of art has a story behind it - from when it was created, to information about the artist who created it. We try to tell those stories, using our website, thedancingrabbitgallery.com, as the vehicle.

The Dancing Rabbit Gallery is an expression of my passion for Southwestern Native American art, and I am very touched by the many comments that I have been receiving recently about our stories. Many of you have asked about our store location, and I have replied that we are only an online store, not a physical storefront. There are advantages and disadvantages to each approach, and my husband Michael and I decided to go the online route.

Our website has lots to offer. The full versions of the stories are there; the ones on Dancing Rabbit Facebook page are shortened versions. We have lots of artist profiles, many of currently active artists who we have been able to meet and develop wonderful relationships. As I mentioned in one of my earlier stories, making friends with artists and learning their stories is what my mother and grandmother did during their lives, and this gives me such a bond to their lives, as well as a bond to my Native American friends.

We also have profiles on the New Mexico pueblos and some of the Southwest Native American tribes. That gives us more context and understanding when we see pictures of the Taos pueblo, in continual use for over a thousand years. It helps us appreciate the work of potters who go into the Jemez mountains and dig their clay from the earth, spending countless hours shaping and creating the incredible pots that we see today; the silversmiths of the American Southwest, who learned their initial skills from the Spanish and expanded those skills through laborious trial and error, to produce stunning bracelets, necklaces, and other jewelry; the skillful weavers of textiles who create both beautiful and useful pieces, often with very intricate patterns; and of the artists who capture the magnificence of the Southwest on paper through paint and photographs.

The website allows each of you to view all of these different items – whichever ones strike your interest – along with the back stories on each item. I have spent endless hours doing research, and relying heavily upon my network of experts, making sure that you see only authentic Native American items with accurate information about them. And there are lots of pictures. If you see an item, but would like a different picture angle, just let me know.

Today's generations are very comfortable with online shopping. If you don't live near the American Southwest, popping in to a Santa Fe or Scottsdale gallery can be a bit of a journey. There are a number of gallery owners in those areas that I know and respect, as they will take the time to give you the back story on each piece they have, and they are fair and honest businesspeople. Many of them have begun embracing the new world of online shopping, and are actually seeing more shopping done online than in their physical stores.

My parents started The Dancing Rabbit Gallery in 1980, well before the Internet was even close to what it is today, and I am working hard to continue their legacy, but also working hard to deliver an outstanding online experience to each of you. I hope that you will continue to share our Facebook page with your friends, visit our online gallery, and give us more feedback as to what you would like to see and how we can make the Gallery website more friendly and useful to each of you.

Adobe Gallery and Al Anthony, Jr.

It is always a wonderful experience when a gallery owner and staff spend time with me, not only sharing the marvelous items they have in the gallery, but also helping me to learn more about my passion, Native American art. In 2013, I had that opportunity recently with Al Anthony Jr., the owner of Adobe Gallery in Santa Fe. He, Scott, and Todd spent hours chatting with me about different pots and artists.

For a while, I have been seeking just the right pot from the Zia Pueblo. Al and Scott steered me toward a magnificent piece by Eusebia Toribio Shije, an award-winning potter who has been winning awards at the Santa Fe Indian Market since the early 1980's.

Al, about to reach his prime at 81, embodies a passion for the beautiful art created by the pueblo people and an appreciation for their lifestyle. He "encourages people to appreciate the nuances of a historic piece of pottery. Smell the clay, feel the shape of the vessel, take in the beauty of the design, and lastly, overlook the scratches and chips of decades of life of the piece."

Originally located in Albuquerque, Al relocated the Adobe Gallery to its current Santa Fe location a few decades ago, where it has happily rested at the foot of Canyon Road, where most of the significant Santa Fe galleries cluster. With his long background in historic and highly valued Native American art, Al has garnered a reputation for immense knowledge and unimpeachable honesty. Michael, of course, loves Al's flair for the perfect Hawaiian shirt, a style he often wears himself.

Adobe Gallery has a wonderful website, but if you are ever in Santa Fe, stop by his gallery at 221 Canyon Road for a real treat. Take your time and just breathe in the ambiance of the gallery, and enjoy your conversations with the guys there.

Katie with Al Anthony, Jr., 2013

A Visit with Kim Seyesnem Obrzut, Hopi Bronze Sculptor

Each May, the City of Southlake and its main shopping area, Town Center, host Art in the Square, a wonderful weekend of artists and their outdoor art. The artists come from all over the world to show their creations in an outdoor venue, sprawled over several acres of the Town Square pavilion area. Each year, Art in the Square grows, and the caliber of artists continues to increase as well.

Last year, my husband Michael and I were strolling the exhibits, peeking in on some of the tents and looking at the amazing talent on display. As we neared the end of one row, we saw some figures that appeared to be nicely carved wood. I was immediately drawn to the tent, and was pleasantly surprised to find out that they were incredible bronze sculptures of Hopi women, with different chemical treatments bringing out different colors on the bronze. The attention to detail was breathtaking, and I found myself enchanted by one particular sculpture, titled "A Place Where the Butterflies Land." When you visit my home page, you can see the sculpture on the carousel of pictures.

Kim Seyesnem Obrzut, Hopi Bronze Sculptor.

As I admired the sculpture, a young lady approached and offered additional information. She was Crystal Obrzut, one of Kim's daughters. She told me some of the story behind the sculpture, particularly the stylized representation of the Hopi women and the cultural significance of the butterflies. And then her mom, Kim Obrzut, came over and we chatted for a bit. Of course, I had to have the sculpture, as it really touched my heart with its graceful lines and stunning majesty. Kim offered to take the sculpture back to Flagstaff so that she could get it cleaned up, and then she would ship it to me. We agreed, and I extended an invitation for Kim and her daughter to come over and visit, breaking some of the tedium of hotel life going from show to show. Time didn't permit that weekend, but we stayed in touch, particularly as this year's Southlake Art in the Square drew near.

The exhibition is a three-day affair, running Friday through Sunday. We made it over to Town Center on Sunday morning, just as they opened at 11 a.m. Crystal was in the tent, and she greeted us both with a smile and a hug. Kim was still back at their hotel, getting things packed for their trip back to Flagstaff. So Crystal showed us some of Kim's newest creations, and we chatted for a bit.

After a while, Kim arrived, and it was almost like two old friends getting together again. In addition to being incredibly talented, Kim is a sweet, wonderful lady and just as gracious as could be. Kim told us stories about the Hopi traditions, and I felt like a little sponge soaking up all of her tales.

Much of Kim's sculpture is taken from her time growing up on the Third Mesa of the Hopi reservation, and she faithfully represents the elegance and serenity of this peaceful people. As Michael and I had driven through the Hopi three mesas earlier this spring, I felt an immediate connection to her stories.

And yes, if you are wondering, I did manage to acquire another of Kim's marvelous bronze sculptures this May, and Kim will be shipping it to me as soon as it is cleaned up and ready for my gallery. I would dearly love to make this an annual tradition, building my knowledge of Hopi and my collection of Kim's work at the same time.

Kim and Crystal have headed back to Flagstaff, with Kim eager to go to California to welcome her new granddaughter to the world in June. Unfortunately, that means we will miss her when we are out in Flagstaff later this month, but I think one of these days we will be able to sit down outside the hubbub of a show and get to know each other better.

After all, that is one of the reasons why I have continued the Dancing Rabbit Gallery – it gives me a wonderful opportunity to get to meet and know some pretty amazing artists. Whether they are painters, sculptors, potters, carvers, weavers, or talented in other ways, I think knowing something about them helps to bring their art to life a bit more for me. Hopefully with these tales of mine, I am able to bring their work to life a little bit more for you as well.

The Spirit of Creation, bronze by Kim Seyesnem Obrzut, Hopi, circa 2014.

Northern Arizona's High Desert and Mountains

A recent trip to Arizona was fairly typical of our journeys and explorations. On this trip we wanted to find out more about the northern part of Arizona, rising from the high desert north of Phoenix to the mountains surrounding the Grand Canyon outside Flagstaff.

A day trip to Casa Grande, located about 40 miles south of Phoenix, started the exploration, as we learned more about the Hohokam tribe, which built Casa Grande and an extensive irrigation canal system along the banks of the Gila River over a thousand years ago. The abandonment of Casa Grande happened about 200 years after they built their settlements, for reasons lost to history but likely involving weather changes and the ability to feed a large centralized civilization. The Hohokam diaspora contributed to the Hopi, Zuni, and other settlements being founded in the high desert and mountains to the north and east.

Casa Grande Ruins National Monument.

After stopping in at the Heard Museum in Phoenix, and visiting with some of our friends in the many Scottsdale galleries, we set off to the high desert. The terrain steadily rises from a barren desert to a thriving, high-altitude, and arid beauty. Technically part of the Colorado Plateau formation, it contains quite a few National Parks and monuments, extending from Utah through Colorado, Arizona, and New Mexico. The centerpiece of the region is the Grand Canyon, which I will get to shortly.

The signature characteristic of the high desert is the saguaro cactus, and we were fortunate enough to catch them in the early part of their annual bloom. As we moved further north, the altitude continued to increase, and we transitioned from high desert to the tree-covered foothills and valleys of the southern Rocky Mountain range. The animals are remarkably adapted to the terrain and weather, as exemplified by the cactus wrens that carve out hollows in the saguaro to build their nests.

From there, Michael and I drove north to Montezuma Castle and Montezuma Well, two locations where some of the Sinagua people (closely related to the Hohokam) settled. Montezuma never actually came anywhere close to Arizona, but early American explorers named them for the Aztec ruler presumably to stimulate tourism. The Castle (a National Park) is a set of cliff dwellings, where the settlers carved out caves from the sides of cliffs, some of them 70 or more feet above the base of the cliff. The settlers would use adobe bricks to construct walls and create living spaces. During the day, the people would go down ladders to the valley floor where they farmed and went about their daily lives. We sat on benches in the shade of large Arizona Sycamore trees and gazed upon the cliff dwellings, recreating in our minds the daily lives of those people over ten centuries ago. It is a peaceful, tranquil site, and the National Park Service has done a remarkable job of preservation of this ancient site.

About 11 miles to the northeast of the Castle area, Montezuma Well is a large natural limestone sinkhole, also in the Verde valley. It is close to four hundred feet wide, and quite deep. It is estimated by the National Park Service that about 1.5 million gallons of water rise into the well each day, draining the Verde valley area and taking up to 10,000 years to soak into the ground and emerge at Montezuma Well, flowing into the Beaver Creek area for Native Americans to grow crops. Many Native American peoples, including the Yavapai and Hopi peoples, trace their origin stories to this site, and it has a special religious connection to them. It is a short walk up the hill to the viewing area of Montezuma Well, but as always in wilderness areas, watch where you step unless you accidentally disturb a desert lizard or other critter.

I will continue writing about this wonderful adventure in the next story, as we visit some of the towns in Northern Arizona, including some of the museums and galleries we visited, fantastic art shows, and of course, the Grand Canyon.

Montezuma Castle National Park, AZ.

Northern Arizona – Towns, Museums, and Serendipitous Discoveries

This story continues the journey that Michael and I took earlier this year, exploring the towns and museums of Northern Arizona…

The first thing that you notice about this area is that it takes your breath away – literally. The altitude rises to over 6000 feet, and for those of us who live much closer to sea level, it is quite a change. The second thing you notice is also breath-taking – the natural beauty of the mountains, valleys, massive stands of timber, and other aspects of nature at its best. Everywhere you look, there is another postcard moment.

We began one morning leaving from our Scottsdale hotel to the lovely town of Prescott. We headed there because the Phippen Museum was hosting its annual Native American art festival, partly located in the Phippen and mostly located on Prescott's tree-lined downtown courthouse square. In addition to the adjacent Yavapai-Prescott Native American lands, artists from around the Southwest swarm to downtown Prescott for a great weekend of festivities. While there, we saw Kim Seyesnem Obrzut of Hopi and her daughter Crystal, and of course I just had to get another of Kim's magnificent bronze sculptures. As with most of our acquisitions, we found that Kim happily shipped from her gallery to our home.

The next stop was another National Park Service site, Tuzigoot. A three-story pueblo ruin built on a hilltop, the structures comprise about 110 rooms and were built by the Sinagua people about a thousand years ago. A fascinating feature of the Tuzigoot structures is the use of trapdoors in the ceilings instead of doors in the walls, providing additional security for the residents. The hilltop has a commanding view of the Verde River valley below, where the Sinagua peoples farmed.

We then headed to nearby Clarkdale, which was founded a hundred years ago due to extensive copper mining in the area. About sixty years ago, the copper mining ceased, and the economy of Clarkdale went into hibernation. Recently, however, the towns of Clarkdale and nearby Jerome are emerging as artist centers, and the old Spanish Colonial architecture of the downtown business district is coming alive once more.

Our first stop in Clarkdale was quite by accident. We entered Clarkdale and immediately saw the old two-story Clarkdale High School. What was unusual, however, was the large copper distillery kettle outside the school.

Copper Museum, Clarkdale, AZ.

Our curiosity aroused, we pulled over and discovered a hidden gem. The high school had been converted, over the past two years, into the home of the incredible Arizona Copper Art Museum.

We went into the Copper Museum where we were warmly met at the front door by the owner/curator of the museum, Drake Meinke. He told us how the Museum celebrated everything copper: from military usage, to kitchen and drink usage, to art and architecture. We knew from our own high school days that Arizona was known as the Copper State, but this Museum really drove home the many uses of copper found in European and American lives. The Museum has different categories in each of the former classrooms, and each separate gallery could easily take hours to view.

Art at Four Eight Wineworks Cooperative, Clarkdale, AZ.

Next door to the Copper Museum, we found a nice little wine bar, Four Eight Wineworks. The bar is a cooperative venture of a number of local, starting winemakers who are experimenting and producing some very nice wines. We were delighted to find a nice tasting menu, so we each got a different flight (so we could share and taste twice as much, of course) and a very tasty cheese and crackers tray.

They had a young lady, Tara Lynn Walrus, singing and playing her guitar, and the small comfortable setting was just what we needed after a long, dusty day of exploration.

After picking out our favorites, we sat for a while with the managing director, Joe Bechard and talked about the co-op founder, Maynard Keenam of Caduceus Cellars, and his efforts to work with the Yavapai College to boost the winegrowing industry in Arizona. Of course, we ended up having a case of our favorites shipped back to our home.

It became a long day, so we happily piled into our car and drove to our comfy hotel room, chatting about all that we had seen and learned that day, and planning for the adventures facing us in the next few days to come.

Northern Arizona and the Grand Canyon

Midway through our recent adventure, we relocated from our hotel in Scottsdale to a different hotel in Williams. The town of Williams is a cute little community located on I-40 to the west of Flagstaff, and is where the main turnoff to the Grand Canyon is located.

There are many ways to get into the Grand Canyon National Park. We found one of those ways by riding from Williams to the Grand Canyon Visitor Center on the Grand Canyon Railway. An old steam engine, converted to run on used french-fry oil, pulls a number of cars each morning up to the Grand Canyon depot, and returns that afternoon. On the ride, there is entertainment, beverage and food service, and lots and lots of magnificent scenery. Elks in particular are plentiful as the train nears the Grand Canyon, and parents and kids alike gleefully point out their sightings.

We wanted to go to the Grand Canyon for many reasons. Among them, learning more about the Native American peoples who still live in this area, and who treasure the canyon and its surrounding areas as part of their creation stories. The Tusayan Ruins, a few miles west of Desert View, show how the ancient Puebloan peoples lived over 800 years ago, though archaeologists have found traces of peoples living in the area for the past 12,000 years.

Though the South Rim is over 7000 feet in altitude (and the North Rim is over 8000 feet), the ancient Puebloan peoples were able to farm and hunt in this area, making use of the bounty provided by nature. Yucca leaves were often woven into baskets and shoes, and deerskin was tanned for clothing. Summer rain, combined with the Colorado River at the bottom of the mile-deep canyon, provided for their agricultural needs.

Hopi House at Grand Canyon National Park, Arizona.

Today, the Hualapai and Havasupai peoples still live at the canyon, and the three mesas of the Hopi are nearby to the east. The large Navajo Nation abuts the Grand Canyon National Park, and is the only part of Arizona that observes Daylight Savings Time. So there are many different ancestral links to the Grand Canyon, and the National Parks Service has tried to preserve and help us interpret these links. The Hopi House, reflecting the incursion of Anglo tourists to the Grand Canyon, was built in association with the Fred Harvey Company to give a stereotypical perspective of Hopi (and by association, Puebloan) history. Interestingly, the Hopi House was designed by a female architect, Mary Jane Elizabeth Colter, and constructed primarily with Hopi workers using natural local materials similar to what the Hopi built for themselves.

Another Anglo tourist feature of the Grand Canyon historic district is the El Tovar hotel, also built at about the turn of the century. When it was finished, many considered it one of the most elegant hotels west of the Mississippi – though at the time, there may not have been many competitors for that honor! The hotel has about a hundred rooms, and is typically fully reserved in the spring, summer, and fall seasons a year in advance.

One of the gems of this rustic hotel is the restaurant. We had a wonderful lunch there one day – the Navajo taco and "El Tovar" chili were truly outstanding. A word of warning – the desert tray will really give you some difficult decision moments, as all the items are sinfully appealing.

El Tovar Hotel at Grand Canyon National Park, AZ.

After a leisurely repast, Michael and I strolled along the South Rim, taking in the views between the El Tovar Hotel and the Bright Angel trailhead leading down into the canyon. The National Park Service also runs three shuttle bus routes, taking visitors to the far western portion of the South Rim, to the far eastern portion where the main parking areas and Visitor Center are located, and in-between among the various parts of the historic district.

Grand Canyon National Park, Arizona.

The views of the Grand Canyon are stupendous, and it is truly amazing what Mother Nature can do with a bit of water and lots of time. The true gem of the canyon, however, is learning about the ancestral Puebloan peoples who lived here for millennia, and how they interacted with the canyon. When you are there, make sure that you have comfortable walking shoes, drink plenty of water, and remain aware of the high altitude. Then you can focus more on the beauty and grandeur of the Grand Canyon, and understand why it is so revered in the stories of the ancient Puebloan peoples who settled this area.

Next up – a side-journey to Flagstaff and the Museum of Northern Arizona.

Northern Arizona – Flagstaff and More Artists

Even in May, the San Francisco mountain range remains snow-capped, giving Flagstaff a beautiful backdrop. The high 7.000 foot altitude and crisp mountain air, laced with the scent of dense Ponderosa Pines, are quite a contrast to the more agrarian area in which we live.

Our main purpose for visiting Flagstaff was to drop by the Museum of Northern Arizona, which has an amazing Native American exhibition, and retrieve two pieces of David Dawangyumptewa's art, which he had been showing for several months as part of a two-artist exhibition. We thought we might stop in on Saturday and coordinate with the museum curators, so that picking up the artwork on Tuesday would go smoothly. As is often the case with our trips, we very fortuitously came at the same time as the Zuni Artist Market, held that weekend at the museum.

San Francisco Mountains, Flagstaff, AZ in May.

For several hours, we happily wandered through the halls of the Museum, greeting a number of our Zuni artist friends, and introducing ourselves to others we had not yet met. The Peynetsas were there, with their stunning owl pottery, and the Quams had a lovely display of their hand-carved fetishes. For me, however, finally getting to meet Bobby Silas and talk with him about his very traditional approach to historic pottery was one of the highlights of the Museum stop. Bobby concentrates on very complex and intricate patterns from the time of the Anasazi and Mesa Verde cliff-dwellers, capturing the elegance and symbolic meanings from the ancient peoples who preceded the current Pueblo Indians.

Though not a large metropolitan area, Flagstaff has a wealth of recreation and tourist activities. We managed to visit the Lowell Observatory, built in 1896 and the discoverer of Pluto in 1930, Meteor Crater, and the historic and quite unique Riordan Mansion.

The Riordan Mansion, a stunning example of the emerging Arts and Crafts style, was built in 1904 by two brothers, who built two almost identical homes joined in the middle by a common living room area. The two brothers married, raised their families in the homes, and were quite instrumental in the development of many of Flagstaff's current amenities. Small group guided tours are available, and we highly recommend that you spend a couple of hours exploring this amazing structure. Not surprisingly, the architect of the Riordan Mansion is Charles Whittlesey, who also designed the Grand Canyon's gorgeous El Tovar Hotel.

Riordan Mansion, built in 1904.

Restaurants abound in Flagstaff, many with live music, as the artist element is very prevalent in this "college-town." Though the population is only about 70,000, Flagstaff has quite an impressive wealth of culture. There are many discoveries that we simply didn't have time to pursue on this trip, like the Naval Observatory and the World Clock, nearby rock-walled pueblos at the Wupatki National Monument, Route 66 nostalgia, white water rafting, jeep tours, the nearby rugged beauty of Sedona, and many more adventures. Future adventures await us!

Our time in northern Arizona was amazing, and our explorations just managed to scratch the surface of this undiscovered part of the United States. We returned to Texas, weary and yet exhilarated, fondly stowing away the memories of this trip and eagerly anticipating the next one.

Zuni Fetishes

Handmade animal carvings (those made by the Zuni Pueblo people of New Mexico) are called Zuni Fetish Carvings. These Zuni fetishes have been with us since before recorded history. Zuni Fetishes are used by shaman to heal the sick and dying. They are carried by travelers to help assure safe passage. In general, Zuni fetishes are meant to bring their owners good fortune and prosperity.

Many people believe that living creatures have a spirit. The Zuni believe that these spirits transition from one form to another, and that they reside in our natural world as rocks while waiting for new life. The best Zuni Fetish carvers can see these spirits and carve the rock in such a way as to release the spirit from the host stone. Sometimes the spirit is so clearly visible in the rock that anyone can see it and that is called a concretion.

Fetishes of Zuni Pueblo carvers

Zuni fetishes are an animal, bird or figure hand carved from stone, shell, antler, wood or other natural materials. Zuni fetishes were first carved as "hunting" fetishes. When taken on a hunting expedition, fetishes would ensure a plentiful and successful hunt. Each fetish is believed to have a spirit within it. If treated and taken care of properly, Zuni fetishes will help guide you on the right path of life. When you purchase a Zuni Fetish or are given one it is your responsibility to care for and treat it with the proper respect it deserves. "Offerings" are often attached to the fetish by the artist; however, you may make your own "offering" to your fetish by attaching a small stone or feather adornment. An offering to your fetish is greatly appreciated and you will be rewarded with the healing or strength you desire. We cannot guarantee that a fetish carving will change your life, but in many years of experience many people have seen astonishing changes in lives as a result of the belief in the power of the fetish. Our fetishes are Zuni carved unless otherwise noted, out of a variety of stone and shell. Fetish prices will vary depending on detail, artist and the medium used.

Prized for their "down to earth" beauty and spiritual renewal, fetishes have long been an important part of Native American culture. When a fetish maker prays over his/her created work, a mystical power is believed to be released which can assist one in finding a solution to any present problems. All Southwestern tribes make and use fetishes; however, the Zuni people have developed a reputation for being skillful fetish carvers. There are six cardinal guardian fetishes which are symbolic of the six directions. The first is a mountain lion which represents the North. The South belongs to the badger, the West to the bear, while the East goes to the wolf. Additionally, the mole guards the inner earth, while the eagle protects the heavenly regions.

Turquoise Hummingbird
by Adrin Cheama

Zuni fetishes are animal carvings that have been used by the A:Shiwi (The People) for over a thousand years. By honoring the animals and acknowledging their special "medicine" (their natural traits), we may summon our own similar attributes.

Fetishes are sometimes used that way today. We can focus on the qualities we have that are like a certain animal. We can carry a fetish with us or keep it on a bedside table. Fetishes may be used to discover, enhance, or simply remember a connection with nature. Each of us has our own reason for taking care of a fetish. Be mindful and respect the spirit of the animal that your fetish represents.

The Zunis feel that it is the spirit within the fetish that is of value, not the object itself. The Zunis regard ceremonial fetishes in carefully dictated ways, while no strict guidelines apply to non-ceremonial fetishes.

The Zuni people believe the spirit of the animal and its power (its strength, cunning, vision and other properties, as well) can become theirs by exchanging breath with the stone carving - exhaling into its mouth and drawing in breath from the mouth of the carving. It is through this process that the owner can have the strength of a bear, the vision of an eagle, and the power of a mountain lion...

L-R : Katie with Kateri Sanchez, Zuni carver,

Lapis Corn Maiden by Sandra Quandelacy,

Picasso Marble Bear by Jeff Shetima

Southwestern Volcanoes

The Pacific Rim, land masses surrounding the Pacific Ocean, include the Pacific states of America, western Mexico, western South America, and across to Japan, China, Indonesia, and so on. The Pacific Rim is noted for frequent volcanic eruptions, as seen in the Mount St. Helens eruption in Washington State, current eruptions in Alaska and Hawaii, and others on a frequent basis throughout the Pacific Rim countries. However, we rarely think about volcanoes as part of the American Southwest landscape.

In March, as Michael and I returned home from the Heard Museum Indian Market in Phoenix, we had a chance to stop at the Sunset Crater volcano to the northwest of Flagstaff. We were surprised to read that this volcano had erupted less than a thousand years ago (1064-1065 A.D.), while the area was inhabited by Native Americans.

As we drove up to the crater overlook, we saw fields of lava with grasses and trees trying to find cracks in which to plant roots and take hold. As this is a National Park Service site, stopping at the side of the road and taking lava rock souvenirs is not permitted. However, we have often noticed the prevalence of lava throughout Arizona, Utah, Colorado, and New Mexico, often coming up to the side of the road. In fact, Interstate 40 across New Mexico cuts through an extensive lava field for quite a few miles.

Sunset Crater, Arizona.

We noted this abundance of volcanoes in an earlier story, with a trip up to the Jemez Pueblo and through the Valles Caldera, a super-volcano. Recently, we did some additional investigation, and found that there are over 1400 volcanoes in the American Southwest, excluding the Pacific states of California, Oregon, and Washington State. These include the San Francisco Peaks outside Flagstaff, Steamboat Springs in Nevada, the Zuni-Bandera field in southwestern New Mexico, and Dotsero volcano in Colorado. Each of these four is relatively close to a population area, but only Steamboat Springs is seen as a high threat for eruption. Most of the 1400 volcanoes, like the Valles Caldera super-volcano, are viewed as dormant or very low risk of eruption.

As we drove through the Colorado Plateau, often among the Navajo Nations lands, we noted a lot of tall cinder cones dotting the land. The near-term threat of volcanic eruption is most likely from these types of cones, similar to the Sunset Volcano crater eruption, which would probably only impact an area of a couple hundred square miles around the eruption site. Fortunately, the U.S. Geological Survey has established a seismic monitoring network throughout the American Southwest and is tracking potential eruptions.

Early Americans recognized the lethal power inherent in volcanic eruptions. But they also recognized that the lava fields could be beneficial in many ways as well. Sharp pieces could be used to skin animal hides, or become ax heads for chopping timber and plants. Pulverized lava could be used as pigment on pots. Pointed pieces might even be used as knives or arrowheads for hunting. And when a volcano began to erupt, they wisely relocated to safer lands.

The land is alive beneath us. Often, it moves in long time cycles that are beyond our conscious recognition, such as the millions of years of uplifting the Rocky Mountain range, or the millions of years of carving out the Grand Canyon. Sometimes, however, the land moves quickly and explosively, letting the heated magma bubble up from below to spew out on the land. The land has massive strength, often subtle, and sometimes violent. As humans, we are only on the land for a short time, a mere instant in geological terms, and we are of the land. We should be wise stewards and caretakers of the land, carefully using the resources and bounty that it provides, and preserving the beauty of the land for future generations. Learning more about the land is but one small step in this long journey.

Sunset Crater National Park, Arizona.

Education is the process of cultivating the imagination.

Fall Begins to Emerge

To the north and east of Santa Fe, the Santa Fe Mountains loom. Technically, they are part of the Rocky Mountain chain, but I like to think of them as a little bit of heaven brought down to the earth. As the summer wanes and fall emerges, changes are taking place in the Santa Fe Mountains.

The leaves of the aspen begin their colorful transition, showering the forest floor with their splendor. Most aren't aware that when they see a stand of aspen, they are actually seeing one living organism that has existed for possibly thousands of years, with only the emergent roots of this organism being the aspen trees that we see. A big stand of aspens is gorgeous, and it is all one big plant.

The pinon scent in the Santa Fe National Forest is pervasive, creating a clear, crisp scent that takes me back to my youth, when my Mother would take pinon branches through the house in the winter to add its natural perfume to the air. Even today, when Michael and I sit on the patio and put a pinon log on

Santa Fe National Forest, New Mexico.

the fire pit, the wonderful aroma brings a smile to my face and sends memories skittering across my mind.

The animals, sensing the arrival of winter, begin their preparations. The images of these animals are faithfully captured by Native American artists with their fetishes, painting, pottery, and other media. A chubby little rabbit, hiding from the raptors swooping above, darts from brush to brush. A furry-tailed squirrel dashes home, a nut firmly in his cheeks. From time to time, larger animals emerge to view their domain, proudly silhouetted against the nearby trees. The Native Americans interpret the spirit of each type of animal, such as the protector eagle or the fierce badger, and often express these attributes in their art.

Fall is my favorite season of the year, as nature's beauty reaches a crescendo of color and sound. The Native Americans strive to live in harmony with nature, rather than trying to overcome and dominate it. They see themselves as sharing this earth with flora and fauna, and respectfully give thanks to the spirits of the plants and animals they harvest for their sustenance. I try to do the same with my own living spaces, and Michael and I have tried to create an oasis of safety and comfort in our living spaces. The birds and critters are frequent visitors, as we live less than a mile from a large lake, and we try to welcome them with food and shelter. The plants are carefully nurtured, yet allowed to grow in their natural form. In this manner, we try to honor Mother Nature, and model the peaceful behaviors of our Native American friends and neighbors.

Shortly, the earth will slumber for a few months, covered by snow and the darkness of short days. But this cycle of life will continue, and the snow will depart and the earth will warm once again, giving birth to new generations of plants and animals. Today, however, go to the Santa Fe Mountains (or wherever you can go to experience the beauty of nature) and take a deep breath. Look around at the wonder of the landscape, and imagine living in cooperation with the land. Watch the clouds, listen to the bird song, and feel the breeze caress your skin. Today, be alive.

Thanksgiving and the Lowden Pot

As we get ready to share Thanksgiving with our family and friends, I want to share this little pot with you as it depicts the bond and curiosity of friends.

These pots are reflective of the stories of little boys (and their pets) going to the rain-collection cisterns atop the Acoma pueblo and doing whatever little boys do. They talk, they laugh, they tell stories, and enjoy the cool waters of the cistern.

It is a miniature from Acoma signed by Lowden. I believe this is Mary Lowden, as she is known for her miniatures. This small pot has four little friends peering over the rim gazing down at three tiny turtles. Each of the children has a ball, a slingshot, or a canteen in their hands or pockets. The dog is just precious hanging on the rim looking with the children down at the turtles - I wonder what he thinks.

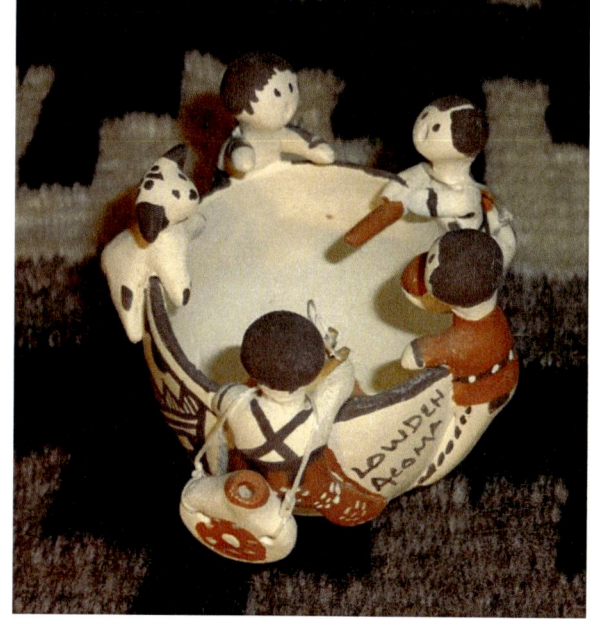

Acoma Story Bowl, either Mary or Virginia Lowden.

The detail achieved by Lowden is wonderful. The canteens are so tiny and precise. The sling shots have strings, in case one wants to shoot at something. The painting on the children's clothing is quite detailed. This little pot with friends gazing at turtles always brings a smile to me.

The Acoma pueblo is located atop a steep mesa in southwestern New Mexico, and there are no natural water sources atop the mesa except for these cisterns. The other alternative is to carry water up the hand-cut steps ascending to the steep mesa, which is what was done prior to the road being built in the past century. The cisterns are still in use today.

Virginia has continued the family tradition, and I was recently able to acquire one of her turkeys for Thanksgiving, and hope to continue this tradition for years to come.

Anita and Virginia Lowden, Santa Fe Indian Market, circa 2015.

Thanksgiving is about families, and started centuries ago in this country as an expression of Native Americans and immigrant Europeans gathering to share the bounty of Mother Earth.

I hope this Thanksgiving will bring a smile to you and yours.

Cluster work – Magnificence in Native American Jewelry

Jewelry has been made and worn in the Southwest since prehistoric times. Native Americans were introduced to metal by the Spanish. For years they acquired metal ornaments through trade, and it was not until the middle of the 19th century that Navajo and Zuni artisans learned metalwork from Mexican blacksmiths and silversmiths. Their early silver jewelry creations were very plain and decorated with simple designs.

Turquoise was first used in silver around 1880. The Navajo and Zuni styles diverged in the early 20th century. The Navajo became known for their use of silver, emphasizing silver-heavy designs with only a few gemstones, while the Zuni focused on stone work, featuring finely cut clusters of gems in complex patterns known as "cluster work".

Cluster work is a jewelry style that is unique to the Zuni people. Although early Zuni jewelry resembled Navajo silverwork, in the 1920s and 1930s Zuni artisans developed a signature style that involved setting large groups of hand cut gemstones into extremely intricate settings. The finely cut gems were often arranged in beautiful patterns that resembled flowers, snowflakes or wagon wheels.

Zuni cluster work is most closely associated with turquoise, although jet and coral, and other gemstones may be used. **Petit point** and **needlepoint** are two types of Zuni cluster work and can be distinguished by the shape and size of the gemstones. **Petit point** refers to gems cut into round, oval, rectangle, pear or square shapes, while **needlepoint** refers to gems that have been cut into a thin sliver or needle shape.

Zuni cluster jewelry, various vintages.

Cluster work is an extremely time-consuming process and fewer and fewer artists are taking the time to hand cut their gemstones. A true piece of Zuni cluster jewelry is an exquisite piece of wearable art that showcases the unmatched lapidary skills of Zuni artists and will be an heirloom for generations to come.

Adapted from *Native American Jewelry Guide* and The Indian Pueblo Cultural Center

Christmas Stories

In an earlier story, I talked about storytellers, and the significance that they hold in the Native American culture. Oral traditions, memories, and culture are all passed from one generation to the next in this way. I hope that in some small way, my blogs honor all the storytellers who have woven this wonderful tapestry of Native American life. Sometimes my blogs are about people, events, and adventures, and sometimes about precious memories from my past. This blog is one of the latter.

The coming of winter is a time for reflection and sharing. The sun peeks above the eastern horizon, casting a bright gaze upon the earth for a while, but then quickly retreating to the west. The animals prepare for their winter slumbers by storing foods, and the trees and plants await the cold and snow. We humans also prepare, setting a brisk fire in the fireplace, drinking warm beverages, and bundling in warm blankets. This is when many of the family stories and traditions are shared from the elders to the young ones.

Christmas stories are particularly poignant in my life, as many of my most precious childhood memories revolve around this holiday season. My father always used to gather his children next to the Christmas tree each Christmas Eve, and read the Christmas story to us from the Bible. Mom would tell us stories of Native American holiday traditions, and we absorbed these traditions as part of our culture. At this time of year, I particularly miss my parents, but I am comforted by knowing that their memories stay alive within me, and are passed along in the stories that Michael and I tell to our children and grandchildren. This is the way of the world.

So each Christmas, I try to share with you a story or two about the holidays. These will include stories about our Southwestern Christmas tree, tasty biscochitos, glimmering farolitos, treasured nacimientos, and more. Please feel free to browse and share the stories, and add your own special memories if you wish. Yes, we still have the storytelling contest running through the end of the year, and your stories and special memories are very welcome as entries.

Through sharing stories, we preserve the traditions of the past. But we also get to know each other better, gaining an appreciation and respect for the commonalities and differences of each other's lives. The more we understand of others, the less we fear the differences, and that opens the door to peace and harmony.

In all of our travels throughout the American Southwest, and throughout the world, that is one constant we have seen among all peoples – the desire to raise their families in peace. So in this holiday season, smile at a stranger, say hello to a neighbor, give a friend a big hug, or share a story with someone. This will bring warmth to your life and to theirs – what a wonderful gift during the cold winter!

Nacimiento – Native American Nativity Sets

We always had a nativity set at Christmas – very traditional in my family. When my mother became friends with Ivan and Rita Lewis back in the '70's, she purchased a nacimiento from them – a beautiful Cochiti set. From then on, it was always a part of our Christmas tradition as well. Mother would set up the traditional nativity in the living room and then set up the Cochiti nacimiento in the family room with the Southwest tree. The traditions easily blended. Every year, my sister lovingly sets up this Cochiti nacimiento in her home, bringing back those wonderful memories.

Christmas has great significance in Native American Pueblo culture, resulting from the ancient influence of Spanish missionaries. A fusion with the equally strong tradition of pottery-making has created the delightful holiday tradition of pottery nativity sets to celebrate the birth of Jesus.

Since the 1970s, Native American nativity sets have been popular with collectors as highlights of their Christmas decorating theme. These popular folk art pottery sets feature the Christian celebration of the birth of Jesus with a decidedly Native American twist. Often the participants in the nativity have the appearance of Native Americans, with the "chonga" bun hairstyle for women or the wrapped braids for men, wearing Indian blankets or clothing, and offering traditional Native American foods like Indian bread, small game animals, a bowl of chiles, or corn. The animals near the manger may be those familiar to Native Americans, like deer, elk, bears, or my personal favorite, rabbits. By making the participants more familiar to them, the Native Americans honor the Anglo nativity set, and also make the nacimiento more meaningful to their lives, a very successful blending of traditions.

Paul and Dorothy Gutierrez, husband-and-wife artists from Santa Clara Pueblo, were among the first potters at Santa Clara to create Native American nativity sets. The couple is also known for their award-winning animal figures and storytellers. They began making nativity sets in about 1970. Paul and Dorothy work as a team, with Dorothy forming the figures and Paul doing the polish and finishing work. Every step, from gathering clay to firing outside, follows traditional Santa Clara methods. "They come out different each time, with different faces. It's nice," Paul relates.

Today, a lovely Santa Clara nacimiento sits on my desk in the gallery to remind me of the true significance of the holiday – and the family traditions that are so important to me. Their seven-piece set is executed in stone-polished and matte-black slip. The pieces include Mary, Joseph, Baby Jesus, two Angels, a cow, and a donkey.

Joseph's and Mary's faces have been minimally sculpted, yet are charmingly expressive and left matte, to contrast with the polished areas. The winsome cow and donkey are highly polished, except for the donkey's mane. The folds of the figures' robes are a simplified, graceful, and yet realistic detail. The Christ Child is snugly swaddled inside the cradle board, with only the head showing, and all are singing robustly in praise, along.

Nacimiento set, Paul and Dorothy Gutierrez, Santa Clara Pueblo, circa 1990.

The combination of stone-polished and matte-finish on the various pieces is the typical look Dorothy and Paul Gutierrez are famous for creating. You can hardly resist stroking the rounded, gleaming black surfaces, they are so tactile.

I look forward to adding to my collection of nacimiento sets, displaying them throughout our home each Christmas season. As with the Southwest Christmas tree and farolitos, the nacimientos are a visible symbol of Christmas and a natural opportunity to share traditions with our grandchildren.

Time stops for no man.
It just seems to slow down a lot when in-laws are visiting.

Christmas Celebrations

Christmas is a time for celebration, reflection, and family traditions. These traditions are passed from generation to generation as a way of preserving memories and customs. My parents visited with artists for many years not only during Santa Fe's annual Market, but in their homes, as well as in my parents' Santa Fe home. This led to many wonderful friendships with many of the noted Native American artists from the past 75 years. I am excited to be making friends now with the children and grandchildren of these friends of my parents. I love to see the traditions continue through the family - through the generations.

One of my mother's dear friends was Carmelita Dunlap of San Ildefonzo Pueblo. Mother would make a special point to visit with her during Santa Fe Market each year, quite often purchasing a piece of Carmelita's incredible pottery. The art of pottery making – in the traditional manner - has been passed down to Carmelita's daughter, Martha Appleleaf. She in turn has taught the traditional way of making pottery to her son, Erik Fender, Than Tsideh (Sun Bird). Martha and Erik collaborate in the making of traditional pottery, just as Carmelita and her aunts did many years ago.

Carmelita was designated a National Treasure during the Nixon administration. She won Indian Market first place twenty times, which is still to date unprecedented. Her daughter, Martha Appleleaf, is the first artist honored with the Southwestern Association for Indian Arts' new Traditional Pueblo Pottery award, which has roots among the potters who helped build the Santa Fe Indian Market - traditional potters. Erik won first place in the 1987 New Mexico Congressional Art at the age of seventeen and in won 1988 first place at Santa Fe Indian Market.

In an article written in 2012, Martha Appleleaf casually reminisced about her family's long line of well-known potters. "I kind of knew what was what with watching my grandmother. She was the one who raised me," Appleleaf said. "They all sat down together polishing — Maria and Aunt Clara and my other aunt. They didn't say, 'Oh, that's your pot or that's mine. They all worked together." Martha and Erik continue to carry on the traditional ways of sharing labor, as well as the techniques of gathering and preparing clay and building, sanding, polishing, painting and firing the pots. Just as her grandmother and aunts would polish together and Martinez' husband Julian would paint her pots, Martha and Erik share various stages of the process. Despite the tremendous skill, patience and hard work traditional pottery requires, Appleleaf obviously loves her art and has instilled that in her son. "It's our privilege and honor that the Clay Mother lets us make her beautiful," she said. "She allows us to do all this to her — and it allows us to have all that we have."

Martha Appleleaf and Katie, Indian Market.

As I have coffee in the Gallery each morning, I look at the family groupings of traditional potters. There are many here, and I am working to identify many of the family linkages among the pottery that I have. This reflection always causes me to ponder the importance of heritage and family traditions. It is through these family traditions and customs that we are able to honor those who are no longer with us and to revere the earth on which we live. Tradition is the pathway from the past, but more importantly, it is the pathway toward a wonderful future for our children.

Remember those who came before us, and give the younger generation a special hug and tell them the stories of their ancestors and their customs. Celebrate and reflect – simply opposite directions of the same pathway. Create that pathway for the young ones and carry on the traditions of family.

From all of us at The Dancing Rabbit Gallery, we wish each of you a blessed Merry Christmas and a safe and healthy New Year.

Erik Fender (Than Tsideh, Sun Bird), San Ildefonso master potter

Clockwise from left: pots by Erik Fender, Carmelita Dunlap, and Martha Appleleaf.

The Story of Farolitos and Luminarias

The lighting of farolitos goes back many, many years in my family. Mom used to set out the paper bags with candles in them each winter, lighting them at dusk and putting them out again as we prepared for bed. It is a wonderful image from my childhood, and I treasure the memories of seeing the beautiful lights flickering in the evening darkness. As an adult, I continued this tradition, but didn't really think about the full meaning and background of luminarias and farolitos.

A traditional luminaria is a small stack of piñon wood, lighting the way for the wise men as they travel through the village to the church. These small bonfires are typically lit on Christmas Eve, celebrating the traditional Midnight Mass and the arrival of the Christ child.

The luminarias have evolved to paper bags with sand to hold them in place, with small candles inside that are lit and protected from the wind by the bags. This led to the term farol, which means lantern. So what we name luminarias today are really farolitos, or little lanterns of paper bags, sand, and candles.

In the Southwest, we see farolitos atop adobe walls, or lining the walkway to the house, guiding the wise men on their way. This led to the use of strings of electric lights atop houses, shining brightly in the Christmas season. Michael and I love to drive around our town in December, looking at the different displays of lights.

It is an even better outing with some of the grandkids in the back of the SUV, as they point and exclaim at the brightly lit and colorful scenes. And every now and then, we see a farolito, or a cluster of them lighting the path, and I am immediately transported back to those simple childhood days of long ago. And now I can share the story of farolitos and luminarias with my grandchildren, and help them connect the dots between luminarias, farolitos, and rooftop lights, and the journey of the wise men as they traveled to Bethlehem.

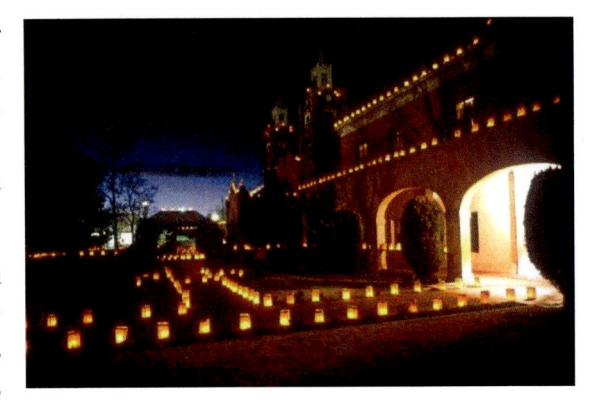

Farolitos illuminate a home.

This Christmas, consider placing a farolito on the porch, or even in the window, and share the story with your family, friends, and neighbors. Traditions are an extremely important part of our culture, and knowing the story behind the traditions, and passing those stories along to the younger generations, is a duty that we each have. These traditions, and the stories behind them, fuel my deep love and respect for the American Southwest, and the peoples and cultures who live here.

From The Dancing Rabbit Gallery, we wish each of you a healthy, happy, and very blessed Christmas!

The Southwestern Christmas Tree

When I was a little girl, my family would decorate our Christmas tree a few weeks prior to the holiday, just like millions of other families around the world. But my mother would always have a second, somewhat smaller tree that she put in the family room on the fireplace hearth. This tree was her Southwestern Christmas tree, and she decorated it with a beautiful collection of Native American ornaments that she had collected on our many trips to parts of the Southwest. The ornaments were typically hand-crafted, made of wood, pottery, glass, and other simple materials. We always thought it was stunning, standing next to the stone fireplace and highlighted by many of the pieces of pottery she had on the family room shelves.

Last year, when I retired from teaching and decided to reopen my parents Dancing Rabbit Gallery as my own, I decided that I needed to have a Southwestern Christmas tree in my gallery. So when my husband and I went searching for a family Christmas tree to place in the front dining room, we also kept our eyes out for the perfect tree for my gallery. And we found one that was amazing.

Many people might overlook a tree like this on the Christmas tree lot, as it wasn't perfectly straight. But it had beautiful branches, was shaped in the perfect pyramid pattern, and seemed to call out to me to take it home. So we did.

Later that day, I showed my mom's collection of ornaments to my husband, and explained the story of decorating a special Southwest Christmas tree each year, and how I had added to her ornament collection over the years, but rarely had the ability to put up a separate Southwestern Christmas tree. Each ornament has a story, like the small pottery ladle or the carved wooden eagle. Each ornament has a special tie to a part of the American Southwest that my parents loved so much. And as I have become wholly immersed in launching this new Dancing Rabbit Gallery, I learn more and more about the culture and the people, and my own love for the American Southwest grows and deepens.

Next week, Michael and I will embark on another search for our family Christmas tree, but we will also be looking for a second tree – the perfect Southwestern Christmas tree that we can decorate while we reminisce. Family traditions are what bind us from generation to generation, and the holiday traditions can be among the strongest ones. I miss my parents, but with this tree, they are never really gone. They stay tucked away in that special part of my heart.

Katie's Southwestern Christmas Tree, circa 2014.

Resolutions for 2016

Every New Year's Eve, for quite a few decades, I have spent a few minutes pondering ways to be a better person in the upcoming year. This is a task done by many people around the world, as the beginning of a new year represents a new beginning and a new opportunity. In fact, recognition of the winter solstice is what led to winter celebrations, decorations, and the holiday season. Centuries ago, the official celebration of the birth of Jesus was moved to coincide with these winter celebrations. And, of course, the recognition of the New Year led to the development of resolutions.

Resolutions are all about self-improvement. For many thousands of years, different peoples have celebrated the New Year by picking one or more areas of their lives that are not satisfactory, and making either a secret or public declaration to improve that area. Improvements are the creation of new habits, or the removal of existing bad habits. Habits tend to take three or more weeks of constant usage before they become part of our behavior, and many resolutions fail because the habits have not yet become ingrained in daily activities.

Sometimes, resolutions can be something simple like smiling at strangers; opening the door for someone carrying packages; or just saying thank you. A resolution can also be larger and stronger, such as making a change in spending habits, personal fitness, or even an attitude adjustment toward family and friends.

Sometimes these changes are painful and are difficult to maintain. Sometimes a breaking point happens. That is when a supportive network of friends and family can help us stay on the right path and repair the breakage faster and with less pain. As with many of us, I have had those breaks occur in my life. We pick up the pieces, and we somehow glue them back together as best we can, and we move on with our lives endeavoring to continue to walk in beauty with nature.

And all of this leads me to my resolutions for the coming year. I am so very blessed with the members of my family and by my wonderful friends, including many in the world of Native American art, both artists and those who support the artists.

I **resolve** to support my friends to the extent I am able, giving encouragement and bringing joy. Sometimes this will be a Facebook like or comment, and other times a shoulder to lean upon. Although I don't have unlimited financial resources, I do have an unlimited heart - as all of us do.

I **resolve** to spread the word of the amazing Native American artists and their breathtaking creations, helping to tell the stories that makes this art so special. They represent a long, vibrant American tradition, and honoring them and their works reflects back on the greatness that this country has become. Without these artists, we would be much diminished.

I **resolve** to continue the struggle against fake Native American art. We have seen a huge inflow of fake art from other countries, passing itself off as made by Native Americans. Jewelry, pottery, textiles, and other areas are all being copied and continue to undermine the efforts of our Native American artists. Yes, it is illegal, and yes, the government is trying to stem the tide, but a knowledgeable buyer walking away from fake art is the best deterrent.

And finally, I **resolve** to redouble my efforts to be involved in Native American organizations, whether it be Facebook groups or events like Indian Market or Native American organizations like SWAIA or IPCC. These organizations are the muscle uniting individual artists and smaller groups of people, giving strength to the goals and objectives of our Native American peoples.

That doesn't mean I will automatically agree with everything proposed, but I do support the right of these organizations to speak clearly and be heard, for that leads to civilized discourse, which leads to resolution of differences. Our country has a great strength in the Native American people, and we must respect different traditions and ways of living, as well as incorporate the Native American threads into the rich tapestry of America. This will make all of us stronger and happier as a result.

Happy New Year, everyone! I pray for each of you successful resolutions in 2016, and a blessed New Year.

National Park Service Preserving Traces of the First Americans

This year is the 100th anniversary of the National Park Service. There are over 411 areas in the National Parks System, including monuments, historic sites, and memorials around our country. Many of these wonderful places feature the evidence of First Americans and their culture.

Archeologists have documented the migrations of many groups of peoples moving into what is now North America. Some of the migrations occurred many tens of thousands of years ago, and the evidence of their settlements is sparse.

But within the past few thousand years, the peoples moving into North America, particularly those in the Southwest part of the continent, began building stronger and more durable structures of the local building materials – mostly stone.

And each of these settlements tells a part of a story – the story of the settlement of North America by the First Americans. Over a thousand years ago, the Casa Grande settlement between modern-day Phoenix and Tucson was built by the Hohokam peoples, involving extensive irrigation canals to grow their crops. Further north, the Sinagua peoples built Tuzigoot, Montezuma's Castle, and similar settlements. In northwest New Mexico, the Chacoan peoples built a massive network of stone settlements in Chaco Canyon, with hundreds of miles of arrow-straight roads facilitating a trading network in the region.

Sometimes, the weather patterns changed and the settlements had to be abandoned. Other times, as was the case of the Sinaguan settlement at Wupatki (Sunset Crater east of Flagstaff), a more dramatic event happened – an exploding volcano a thousand years ago certainly qualifies for that!

Often the settlements have some records – petroglyphs and daily life implements like metatas (corn grinders). But even the records can be open to interpretation. Does the bird symbol mean that it was a local animal, or a spiritual symbol, or just a tasty treat? That is part of the challenge facing the archeologists, who are often aided and sometimes confounded by the current Native American descendants of these ancient peoples.

But there are two existing settlements that go back over a thousand years of continuous occupation. These are the Taos Pueblo in north central New Mexico and the Zuni Pueblo in southwestern New Mexico. Each has a

Metata (corn grinder) in Northern Arizona.

rich and dramatically different tradition. The Taos Pueblo peoples are linked to a Northern Tiwa-speaking culture, and carefully guard their traditions, values, and way of life.

The Zuni Pueblo has also been continuously occupied for over a thousand years, but the Zuni peoples have been in this part of North America for many thousands of years. Unlike other Puebloan peoples, or descendants of the Sinaguan or Chacoan peoples, the Zuni culture evolved largely isolated from other peoples, resulting in a unique language that doesn't have roots in the base languages that many of the Native American tribes and Puebloan peoples speak – Tiwa, Tewa, Towa, Navajo, Apache, etc.

The National Park Service has been working for the past hundred years to preserve the ancient settlements and treat them with the immense respect they deserve for these settlements are the beginning of the story of the North American peoples, with the European invasion only happening in recent history.

Many Native American peoples are working with the National Park Service to help preserve their stories, and many cultural centers and Native American museums work hard to do the same. This effort is necessary, for even if we have no Native American blood in our veins, the First Americans are still a vital part of the story of who we are today. How we preserve, respect, and treasure these elements of our heritage speaks volumes about our value system and culture.

Tuzigoot National Park, northern Arizona.

Small whispers precede the roar of the masses.

The Long and Winding Road

The American Southwest is an incredibly beautiful part of the country. Sweeping vistas, soaring snow-capped mountains, dense forests of trees, stark red mesas, and deep river canyons all bear witness to the power of Mother Earth and the forces of nature at work on the landscape over millions of years. Much of the New Mexico terrain is covered in lava from volcanic eruptions, and this is also seen in the Sunset Crater in Arizona as well. The continental drift produced mountain ranges that displaced a large inland sea, exposing dozens of layers of sedimentary rock strata that provide sharp contrasts as one views them, almost as though Mother Nature had used a wide paintbrush in horizontal strokes. Erosion has also uncovered a number of startling treasures within the land. The Painted Desert and Petrified Forest are vivid examples of the colorful palette that Mother Nature has used in her art.

Last week, Michael and I had a chance to explore a bit of the Southwest as we drove from Dallas to Phoenix for the two day Indian Market at the Heard Museum. As we drove mile after mile, we discussed the challenges of the ancient peoples who moved into this area tens of thousands of years ago, eventually forming communities and finding ways to coexist with the land. The distances in the Southwest are immense, and a two hour drive in a modern automobile might have been two to three weeks of walking back then.

Much of the Southwest is more vertical than horizontal. We spent a week driving up through Payson, where the largest stand of Ponderosa pines in the world grows, and also through Jerome, Sedona, and Flagstaff, where early settlers found old dwellings of the ancient peoples. The National Parks Service has worked diligently to preserve the dwellings, helping us understand a bit more of how these ancient peoples lived and how they evolved into the modern day Native American peoples who live in these areas today.

On previous trips, we have been to Tuzigoot, Montezuma's Castle, and similar Arizona sites of ancient peoples. This trip, we made a special excursion to Chaco Canyon, an immense canyon in western New Mexico that was home to the Chacoan peoples from about 850 A.D. to about 1250 A.D. During that time, the Chacoan peoples built a thriving network of great houses and an extensive stone highway system linking them.

Outside Sedona, Arizona.

Pueblo Bonito and similar structures have been reconstructed and preserved by the Smithsonian, National Geographic Society, and most recently by the National Parks Service. Because of their highway system (two and four lane roads, up to thirty feet wide, and stretching for hundreds of miles), the Chacoan peoples were active traders throughout the region, interacting with many other peoples like the Sinagua.

When we travel through the American Southwest, we see the splendor that Mother Nature has given us. With a little digging, we can learn about the ancient peoples who first lived here, and that helps us understand more about their cultures, beliefs, rituals, and ways of life. In turn, that helps us understand the proud heritage of the Native Americans – both tribal affiliations like the Navajo Nation and Hopi Nation as well as the Puebloan peoples like the Zuni, Taos, and Santa Clara. Each with a strong tradition that links back to their ancient peoples, and each shaped a little differently because of the manner in which their ancestors interacted with Mother Earth. The stories are rich and vibrant, and over the next few weeks we will try to share more stories of some of what we learned on this latest trip through the magnificent American Southwest.

Pueblo del Arroyo, Chaco Canyon.

Chaco Canyon

Chaco Canyon (and the National Parks Chaco Culture National Historic Park) is located in northwestern New Mexico. It is a remote canyon carved out of the New Mexico plains millions of years ago by the Chaco Wash, and served as a major cultural and community center for the Chacoan Peoples over a thousand years ago. The Chacoan peoples built over 15 large dwelling complexes in the Chaco Canyon, mostly between 950 A.D. and 1250 A.D., and established a thriving trade network extending for hundreds of miles around the canyon area. The Chaco ruins are considered to be the ancestral homelands of the Hopi and Puebloan peoples, and are sacred to them. Because of their fragile nature, many of the ruins are kept in a preserved state by the National Park System and available for viewing but not climbing by tourists.

Michael and I had a chance to spend most of a day at Chaco Canyon recently, and we were completely in awe of the detailed planning and construction of these dwellings. The National Parks System has constructed an educational Visitor Center, and put a counter-clockwise loop road through the canyon, allowing visitors to get up close and personal with the pueblos. There are informative maps and guides available, describing the structures and archaeologist speculation as to their uses. At each stop, there is parking, and even restroom facilities at a couple. Be aware that Chaco Canyon is over 6200 feet in altitude, so stay well hydrated and watch out for heat exhaustion.

The central feature of Chaco Canyon is Chaco Wash, flowing through the canyon and actually carving out the canyon over hundreds of thousands of years. The wash formed the wide, flat canyon floor and further provided a meager source of water for the Chacoan Peoples when they settled in the area.

But the history of Chaco Canyon goes back further than the Chacoan Peoples who arrived a thousand or so years ago. The first settlers were the Clovis big-game hunters, meandering through the area over 10,000 years ago. After many thousands of years, the Ancient Puebloans (the Anasazi people in Navajo terms) settled and began the construction of the first pueblos, using the stone from the mesa walls and timber from mountains over 50 miles away. Pueblo Bonito, the largest and most well-preserved of the dwellings is constructed in typical Chaco fashion with

Pueblo Bonito, Chaco Canyon.

a half-moon shaped set of residential dwellings facing a courtyard and ceremonial kiva in the courtyard. Pueblo Bonito, with its approximately 50 residential rooms, could support a population of several hundred people.

All the fifteen major pueblos in Chaco Canyon were constructed to align with solar and lunar cycles, and each maintained a direct line of sight visibility with its neighbors. Chaco Canyon emerged as a major trading area throughout the Southwest, as well as a major center for spiritual and religious activity. To facilitate travel, the Chacoan Peoples built massive roads, arrow straight regardless of obstacles like mesas (they carved steps into the mesas to climb up and down) and wide enough for two lanes of traffic to pass. The road network was labor intensive to build and maintain, and to this day is a marvel of ingenuity and creativity among the Native American construction activities.

Speculation is that a major 50 year drought forced the Chacoan Peoples to abandon their valley, spreading to the southeast and southwest in search of stable water sources. They were succeeded in this area by the Apache and Navajo, and many Navajo live in the area to this day, though the formal Navajo Nation lies to the west. The entire Chaco Canyon site has been deemed a UNESCO World Heritage Site, comprising the largest concentration of pueblo dwellings in the American Southwest.

The story of Chaco Canyon, and the Chacoan Peoples, is a rich chapter in the story of the American Southwest. Many artifacts from Chaco Canyon were removed in the early part of the 20th century and taken to Washington D.C. for exhibition, and are now in the process of being returned to the Chaco Canyon where they can provide in situ testament to the lives of these peoples. The National Park Service continues to work with Native American groups to preserve the knowledge while remaining respectful of the sacred nature of this site to Native Americans. Chaco Canyon contains many of the roots from which today's Native Americans in the Southwest have come, and has tremendous importance for that reason.

Chaco Canyon ruins, Pueblo Bonito.

The Legacy of Margaret Tafoya

Margaret Tafoya is one of the matriarchs of pueblo potters. She recently passed away at the age of 96, but her legacy is enormous. Any gallery or museum that features Native American pottery has one or more pieces done by Margaret, or they dearly wish that they had.

Maybe a bit of the backstory would be helpful in showing context for Margaret's impact. Pueblo pottery has been made in the traditional way for as long as the pueblos have been around, and likely much longer than that. Certainly the Membres and Anasazi potters were making their items well over a thousand years ago, producing daily use vessels for food preparation and storage, water storage, and other utilitarian tasks. Typically the pots were made by the women of the pueblo, as the men either hunted for game or farmed the fields.

Clay for the pots was gathered by hand, digging chunks from the earth and bringing it back to the pueblo. The clay was transformed into long coils and formed into pots, thus leading to the term "hand-coiled" as opposed to more modern ways of molding or using pottery wheels. When the pot was created and the surface carefully smoothed, often the potters would decorate the pots with mineral and vegetable paints, painstakingly applied with yucca fibers as their brushes. The designs were their art, and symbolic of the world in which they lived. After the paint was applied, the pots were fired in an outside pit, using dried woods or animal dung to create the heat needed to cure the pots. Creation of a pot was hard work, and many broke during the firing process, reducing all the hard work to mere shards.

Different pueblos had different sources of clay, and they also used different approaches to decorating their pots. Today, someone who is knowledgeable in pueblo pottery can often identify the pueblo that produced a pot by its clay composition or style.

But the story is even more significant in that pueblo potters passed their knowledge and techniques of making pottery to their children and grandchildren, thus leading to consistent styles that make Zuni pottery distinct from Santa Clara pottery, and so forth.

And that is where we start the story of Margaret Tafoya. The different pueblos began producing commercial pottery around the turn of the 20th century, as Anglo expansion intruded more into their lands with trains and roads. Expert potters emerged in each pueblo, and their pots were more highly sought than those done by other potters of lesser skill. Margaret, having learned the techniques of Santa Clara pottery from her parents, emerged as one of the expert potters and Santa Clara pottery rapidly came to be associated with her.

Margaret Tafoya, Santa Clara matriarch potter.

As often happens, Margaret married and she and her husband started a large family. Each of her children were introduced to pottery at an early age, and some took to it readily while others found different interests. Margaret was very prolific in her potting, and generated a sizeable quantity of very high quality pots during her lifetime. In March, when I had the wonderful opportunity to talk with one of her daughters, Toni Roller, I learned that later in her life, Margaret would often doze as she was potting. Margaret continued potting until she passed away at the age of 96.

Pottery by Toni Roller and her son, Cliff Roller, Santa Clara pueblo.

The legacy of Margaret Tafoya, and her emblematic black bear claw symbol, continues through not only her pots, but the work of her children, grandchildren, and even great-grandchildren who continue to produce award-winning pottery. Toni won so many awards in her earlier days that she stopped entering competitions, letting the other potters win some of them. One of Toni's sons, Cliff Roller, is also a highly acclaimed potter, and his children are beginning to accumulate awards as well.

The tradition of Santa Clara pottery, thrust into international prominence with the works of Margaret Tafoya, is alive and thriving. As I gaze on my pair of Margaret Tafoya pots, next to the Toni Roller pot, next to the Cliff Roller pot, my thoughts automatically trace the Tafoya family lineage, and the pots become so much more special to me. Not only are these pots individually wonderful works of art, but they are collectively the story of a family over several generations, and that gives the pots a wonderful voice to tell a magnificent story. Being able to tell a story such as this is why I collect, and why I try to share these stories with each of you.

And yes, if you are wondering, I will be writing another story shortly about my amazing visit with Toni Roller and her husband at their home in the Santa Clara pueblo. That tale is one that I hope you will all appreciate as much as I enjoyed their gracious hospitality.

The Tafoya Ollas

A while back, I was able to acquire a pair of black Santa Clara ollas (water jugs), each with the emblematic bear claw imprint made famous by the Tafoya potters. The two ollas are gorgeous, each standing about a foot tall and in quite good condition. Unfortunately, they were not signed, as that was not typically done back in the 1920's or 1930's, the estimated vintage of these ollas. However, a pottery expert who I respect tremendously, Mark Sublette of Medicine Man Gallery, has attributed these ollas to "one of only two people in the world who could have made them – either Margaret Tafoya or her mother, Sara Fina Tafoya."

But, without the signature on the pots, I could only call them "attributed to" instead of "made by." Being obsessed with provenance and accuracy, I tried to think of ways to learn the story behind the two pots. "Attributed to" just wasn't good enough for me.

Last year, I was at the Santa Clara pueblo, visiting with one of Margaret's daughters, renowned potter Toni Roller. She and her wonderful husband Ted chatted with Michael and me for over an hour, showing us her studio and taking us on a private tour of her firing area. Ted was so proud of the metal frame he had built to help protect the pots from falling, burning wood and manure during the firing process, and Toni eagerly showed us a new type of tan clay she had found in the mountains near where her family had been digging clay for many decades. It was an amazing time with the Rollers, and I learned quite a bit about Toni's children and grand-children, potters and sculptors developing wonderful talents as well.

While in her gallery, Toni showed me the polishing stones that had been handed down from her mother and grandmother, and that Toni used to this day to smooth the surfaces of the pots before firing. I told Toni about the two pots I had acquired, and she said that it would be easy to tell who made them if she could hold them. This comment was echoed by her son Jeff Roller, while we talked with him later that fall at Santa Fe's Indian Market. So we said yes, the next time we were driving through New Mexico, we would bring the pots for them to see.

Earlier this spring, Michael and I made our preparations to head to Phoenix for the Heard Indian Market, and we carefully packed the two ollas in a large storage bin and put them in the trunk of our car. It seemed like every time we hit a bump, I tensed up and shot Michael an evil look, urging him to avoid the road bumps. During our trip, we went on a number of rugged dirt roads out to the Honanki and Palatki Heritage sites near Sedona, and on the washboard roads to Chaco Canyon. Even State Highways were suspect, as the road surfaces were not nearly enough to soothe my frayed nerves.

But finally, over 3000 miles later, we wound our way up to the Santa Clara pueblo and met with Toni and Jeff. As soon as we took out the pots (and I made sure they were not damaged), Toni picked up one of them and an incredibly happy look came across her face. "My mother made this," she said, "without a doubt." She felt the shape of the shoulders to the olla she was holding, and said that her mother made smoother shoulders, while Sera Fina made taller ones. She put her hand in the olla, and felt the bear claw imprint from the inside. "They used their fingers to press the bear claw in the old days, unlike today when we use a press." And sure enough, I could reach in and feel the impression on the inside of the pot.

But the final piece of the puzzle came when she felt the smooth surface of the pot. Her mother always spent extra time in smoothing the surface before it went to firing, which Sera Fina didn't do as much. And then Toni came to a startling conclusion. "The first pot was made by my mother, Margaret," she said. "But the second pot was made by Sera Fina, and then smoothed by Margaret. And they may have even been made at about the same time, as they are very similar in appearance."

Learning the story of these two pots was invaluable to me. Being there and watching Toni hold the pots that her mother and grandmother had made 80 or 90 years ago, seeing the glow in her eyes and the smile on her face as she looked back on those fond memories, and hearing her tell the stories about her mother and grandmother – that was the real treasure of the day for all of us.

Jeff was kind enough to write out a note with their conclusions about the provenance of the two pots. And then we carefully packed away these two treasures, and also carefully packed away our memories of the visit to the Roller Studio at the Santa Clara Pueblo. My obsession with learning the story of these two was satisfied, but seeing Toni hold the pots gave me even more of a connection to them; much more than just pieces of fired clay.

Pottery by Margaret Tafoya and her mother, Sara Fina Tafoya, Santa Clara Matriarch potters, circa 1930s.

The Agony of the Pot

OH, NO!

Earlier, I wrote about the incredible amount of time it takes to make an authentic Native American pot. Gathering and cleaning the clay, making small coils and forming them into the actual pot shape, trimming and polishing, possibly painting intricate designs, and then firing the pot in the traditional manner. And then, from time to time, the pot cracks in the firing and is useless. Traditional outdoor wood firing generates temperatures of about 1200 degrees Fahrenheit, which is enough to harden the clay and fix the paint, but not to the 2200 degree point which most kilns reach that strengthen the molecular structure of the clay to a very hard pot. However, outdoor wood firing often generates "smoke clouds," which lend a unique beauty to the pots.

My friend Stacey Carr, a wonderful potter from Laguna, recounted an experience he had just prior to Indian Market, when his firing resulted in several cracked pots. The anguish in his voice was clear, as he described uncovering what he thought would be potential blue ribbon award winners, only to find a stack of useless clay. But then he said that this is the life of the traditional Native American potter – sometimes it works well, and other times it doesn't. One learns to deal with the highs and lows caused by the firing process.

A few weeks ago, I acquired an incredibly beautiful lidded pot from Jeff Roller, an accomplished potter from the Tafoya family lineage. Jeff's pots are very traditional, hearkening back to the 19th century for some of his designs. One of the things that makes his pots so striking is that he sometimes makes fitted lids for the pots, a very difficult task. And even more challenging, his lids often have sculpted figures of southwestern wildlife on them. The one I bought had a magnificent detailed ram, standing about 2 inches above the lid.

Jeff was so careful in packing and shipping the pot to me. He actually put the pot in one box, carefully bubble wrapped and enclosed in peanuts, and then put that sealed box in side another one, also filled with peanuts. The lid was done in the same manner, with its own box-in-a-box packing. Both pieces arrived safely, and Michael and I spent the first evening just looking at the beautiful lidded pot as it sat on the kitchen island.

Pot with lid and ram figural, Jeff Roller, Santa Clara master potter, 2015.

I spent a couple of days rearranging parts of my somewhat crowded gallery to give this pot its due honor as one of my most elegant and prized pieces of pottery.

Later in the week, I began the process of taking photos of the pot so I could put it up on the Dancing Rabbit Gallery website. But for some reason, the lighting just wouldn't cooperate with me. I was trying to highlight the magnificent color variations. I moved it from the gallery to the back porch, then to the patio, trying to find just the right combination of lighting and backdrops to give me some great shots that did justice to the textures, incised carvings, and ram sculpture of this fantastic piece of pottery. It was a beautiful sunny fall day, with a breeze blowing from the northwest, but nothing was working for me. Finally, I brought the pot back in the gallery and tried to use a piece of white foam board as a backdrop.

And then, out of nowhere, a gust of wind came blowing through my gallery window, knocking the foam board onto the lid of the vase, and snapping off the sculpted ram from the lid. I froze in shock! This NEVER happens to me. I have never broken a piece of pottery in my life. But there lay the ram on its side, with an accusing gaze in its eyes. My heart stopped for (I think) several minutes, and my stomach lurched about the room. I was literally unable to move for quite a while, just horrified at what had just happened to this incredible piece of art. I, too, have experienced, similar to my Native American potter friends, the agony of pottery. Not an experience I ever, ever wish to repeat.

A couple of hours later, Michael came home from teaching his college students, and I told him what had happened. Of course, being the wonderful and supporting husband that he is, he comforted me and talked me off of the emotional ledge on which I perched. He helped me through the classical four stages of grief – denial, anger, depression, and acceptance, and then we started talking about what to do.

The first action I took was to contact Jeff Roller and let him know about my tragedy. It felt really bad doing that, as part of Jeff's soul is in the art that he creates. Jeff was very comforting, and offered to make a replacement lid for the pot, as the lid and the ram figure on top were the over-the-top elements that made this pot so incredibly special. I am packing up the pot and the lid today, and will ship it to him so he can begin the laborious and time-consuming task of making another lid that exactly fits the pot. I know Jeff will do an amazing job with the new lid – of that I have no concern – but that pot will always be, in my mind, the one that carries the memory of that gust of wind, and the poor defenseless ram lying next to the lid. Hopefully we will have the new lid soon, and I can put this magnificent creation on the Gallery website.

My appreciation and respect for Native American potters has increased once again, as I have a much more visceral appreciation of the soaring joy of a beautiful pot as well as the depths of despair at a broken pot. The life of an artist is not an easy one. Their tears of joy and sorrow are in the work that they give us. It also gives us something to consider the next time we look at a pot, blanket, sculpture, painting, or other Native American art work.

The Ecstasy of the Pot

It finally arrived!

I mentioned a few months ago how I had accidentally snapped the figural ram off the lid of an exquisite Jeff Roller pot, and was crushed at the damage done to this incredible work of art. But, as I also said, I contacted Jeff and he agreed to make another lid with a ram on the lid to replace it. Well, it arrived today!

This is not a simple process on the part of the potter. Jeff's pots and fitted lids are very precise, even to the extent of a carefully hidden notch indicating how the lid is to fit on the pot. So for him to remake a lid meant that he had to have the original pot, and then carefully create a new lid with the ram on it, accounting for shrinkage during the firing process.

Jeff is a very traditional potter from Santa Clara pueblo, having learned the techniques from his mother Toni Roller, and his grandmother, Margaret Tafoya. His aunts, cousins, and siblings all developed their styles in this environment. The clay is dug from the surrounding hills and cleaned and prepared in the traditional manners, and then the pots and lids are painstakingly created, polished, and carved to represent the spirit of the clay within. Jeff's striking style often includes a carved animal figural on the fitted lids, with such dedication to detail that it is easy to see the underlying bone structures, muscles, and even expressions on the animals. One almost expects these tiny animals to come stepping and prancing off of the lids!

So, as I mentioned at the start, Jeff's pot and newly constructed fitted lid with a figural ram finally arrived yesterday. I had been so sorrowful since the accident, and when I carefully unpacked the pot and lid yesterday, those emotions came rushing back to me. You can imagine how careful I was to lift the pot and lid out of the secure packing that Jeff gives to all of his shipments. I gently sat the pot on the kitchen island and slowly put the lid on it in the proper alignment. Then I stepped back and just admired the pot and lid for what seemed like hours. I even think the ram smiled at me once or twice, knowing how much I loved him.

So, Jeff, when I first saw your works in clay and bronze, I knew I had to bring some of them into my Gallery. When I received the first pot with the ram, I was so joyful, only to have that joy dashed when the foam board fell on the ram lid and snapped off the ram. It was agony, indeed. But you were so wonderful to build me another lid, and now my Jeff Roller pot is complete once again. Transferring the pot to an honored spot on my Gallery shelves, sitting and watching the pot last night and again this morning, has helped me to soothe the pain of the breakage, and regain some of the ecstasy that I felt when I first saw your incredible talent displayed in this pot. I collect Native American art, mostly from the Southwest, because it speaks to my soul, and I feel so blessed to have so many amazing pieces in the Gallery. I am also very blessed to get to know some of the wonderful artists who create this art.

Michael asked me this morning, as we had our first coffee in the Gallery, if I had a favorite piece among the many on the shelves and walls. I thought hard about that for a bit, and quickly realized that I really didn't. Each piece has its own quality and story to tell, and I love hearing the pieces tell me their diverse and unique stories. Yes, some pieces have richer or clearer stories, and some pieces do touch my soul more directly. Jeff's pot with the fitted lid and figural ram perched atop certainly fits in that latter group, as gazing at it does take me to another place and even another time. It gives me a window into another culture, and I can catch glimpses of the incredible artistic talent residing in Jeff's soul. That is, after all, why we acquire art. It speaks to us, and tells us its story. Native American art has a multitude of stories, and all we need to do is listen and be enriched.

A Visit with Toni Roller

It was a beautiful March Saturday in Santa Fe. Michael and I had just driven from Tucson to Flagstaff to Hopi to Zuni to Santa Fe, and we were having a great trip meeting with artists and learning more about their lives and art.

After a hasty breakfast, we headed down to the Santa Fe Square to check in on some of our favorite Galleries, like Andrea Fisher and Shalako. We stopped for lunch, then went up to Canyon Road to see our friend Al Anthony at Adobe Gallery. It is a small world, and the gallery owners and artists all seem to know each other, yet they are all so willing to share information and provide guidance and direction. I think that the gallery owners that I enjoy the most are the ones who have a similar approach to lifting up the wonderful works of Native American artists and letting the stories of the artists be heard.

Though I had been to many pueblos in my life, I had not yet made it to Santa Clara, just an hour north of Santa Fe. And because the afternoon was so glorious, we hopped in the car and drove up I-25. Our goal – to visit the Toni Roller Gallery and see some of her award-winning pottery.

Fortunately, Toni's website has very specific and detailed directions, so we were able to find her studio (next to her house) quite readily. We parked, and were met by a gentleman who introduced himself as Ted Roller, Toni's husband. He showed us her Gallery, and regaled us with stories of learning to integrate into a family of potters. Ted was from North Dakota, and ended up in the Santa Clara pueblo after his marriage to Toni.

After a while, Toni returned from her errands and came into the gallery to visit with us. She proceeded to take us back to her workshop and storage areas, and showed us her clays, slips, and firing pit.

Toni still does her pottery in the traditional way, digging the clay from the hills and spending hours transforming it from a rock-like substance into a malleable clay that she can hand-coil into pots. She showed us some of her work-in-progress, and even showed us some of her mother, Margaret Tafoya, and her grandmother, Sera Fina Tafoya. She proudly showed us the works of her children and grand-children, and I think she is very pleased that her teaching is being passed down through the generations of the Tafoya line.

Toni Roller, Santa Clara master potter.

After a couple of hours of chatting with this wonderful lady, my head was spinning and I was somewhat giddy with excitement. It was such an honor to talk to this highly acclaimed artist, and to acquire a pot from her that she just finished. Even better, she personally signed her book *Indian Pottery* for me, and it will go on my reference shelf as one of my treasured possessions.

The pot that I acquired from Toni is magnificent, as all of her work is. But last year, she found a new color of clay next to where her family had been digging for almost a hundred years. This has resulted in a light orange with black speck color of pot when fired, and it is most striking and unusual. She isn't sure how long this new vein of clay will last, so I greedily laid claim to one of the few she had in her gallery.

My Tafoya family tree of pots is more robust. In addition to the two highly-treasured Margaret Tafoya pots, I now have a Toni Roller pot and companion story, plus one from her acclaimed potter son Cliff Roller. Still working on Cliff's siblings. Then on to the next generation, I suppose, with those emerging, talented potters. The pottery tradition runs strongly in the Tafoya family, and the artistic excellence is carefully passed from generation to generation.

Hanging Out at the Heard

Coming up on March 5 and 6, 2016, the Heard Museum in Phoenix will hold their annual Indian Fair and Market. This prestigious event, in its 58th showing, gathers top Native American artists from North America to exhibit and compete. This year, the Heard has over 600 highly talented artists who will be in attendance. The weekend festival is alive with demonstrations from various artists, music, and dance performances, all celebrating the colorful and rich tapestry of Native American life. This year, the main theme is "Celebrating the Art of Pottery" which is certainly an area that I celebrate. And yes, the best part – the artists will have their works for sale at the exhibition as well!

Similar to Santa Fe's annual Indian Market in August, this Market has a full list of activities, both free and paid, that are available to the anticipated 15,000 attendees. There are tickets required for entry to the Heard Museum for this event, but this cost is well worth the opportunity to wander around, talk with the artists, see their stunning works up close, and learn a little more about Native American culture.

Some of the free events that Michael and I always enjoy are the cultural performances. The Grand Entry is a spectacular, colorful entry of Native Americans in ceremonial clothing, with the Thunder Springs Singers drum circle providing a spirited beat. We also enjoy watching the Fancy Dancers, and this year the Oklahoma Fancy Dancers and the Yellow Bird Dancers will be performing, among many other groups.

Heard Museum Indian Market, circa 2015.

Leaving the Amphitheater and moving to the Courtyard Stage, we will hear lovely, sometimes hauntingly beautiful music by Native American musicians, including my favorite, the flute. Also at the Amphitheater, the Zuni Olla Maidens will do the Pottery Dance - dancing while carrying ollas on their heads. Led by Juanita Edaakie and Loretta Beyuka, this very talented group of ten women has performed throughout New Mexico at some of the most notable venues. Their ability to balance beautiful ollas while dancing is amazing!

And, of course, the Hoop Dance, led by Tony Duncan, will allow those brave souls to get out and learn a few of the basic moves of this energetic and popular dance. We will be sure to clap and cheer for you!

One of the not-free events includes Friday night's Best of Show Dinner, in which the award winners for each category are announced, and a drawing for four donated pieces of pottery is held. There is also a silent auction with quite a few pieces available. And yes, these are events that I love, as the award winning pieces are truly quite astonishing.

Proceeds from the Heard Museum Guild's Indian Fair and Market go toward educating visitors about Native American life and culture, helping us to understand more clearly their traditions. The Guild has done significant work to help the Heard Museum and also to organize this amazing event each year.

Hope to see you there one of these days!

Territorial Indian Arts & Antiques Gallery

On a recent trip to Arizona, we had a chance to stop in Scottsdale and visit with Deb and Alston Neal, the owners of Territorial Indian Arts & Antiques Gallery. I had been eager to do so for a while, as I have received a lot of very helpful information and advice from Deb and Alston about some of the items in my gallery that I have been researching. They have been so gracious, helpful, and downright knowledgeable, that I wanted to stop by and meet them in person.

Their gallery has been in operation since 1969, actually started by Alston's mother, who recruited young Alston to work in the gallery while he was still in grade school. He later took over the gallery from his mom, and Deb and Alston have been building quite an enviable reputation ever since.

The focus of this gallery is primarily vintage and antique works, which plays right into their strengths as expert appraisers of Native American arts on PBS's Antiques Roadshow.

Katie with Deb and Alston Neal, 2016.

Even better, after spending some time with Deb and Alston in Scottsdale, they came to Ft. Worth last week to exhibit at Brian Lebel's Old West Show and Auction. Michael and I stopped by and visited with them again, and learned once again how important networking is in this business. It seemed like everyone at the show knew Deb and Alston, and many made a point of stopping by to say hello. With over 200 dealers exhibiting everything from historic rifles and fancy saddles to Native American rugs, pottery, and other art forms, there were a lot of people and a lot of competition. Yet Deb and Alston made time for everyone who stopped by, whether competitor, collector, or just the mildly curious who sometimes wander into these types of shows.

Over the past few years, as Michael and I have traveled about the Southwest, we have had a chance to meet quite a few Native American artists, and have developed solid friendships with many of them. In addition, we have had a chance to talk with other gallery owners, and have found the majority of them to be quite helpful and friendly, even though they know we also have a gallery. There is so much to learn about this small slice of our American culture, and so many wonderful people who are willing to share their knowledge, that it sometimes takes away my breath. Those special moments of knowledge, or special friendships, are what life is all about, and I feel fortunate to be able to travel this path.

Retrospective on the 2016 Indian Market at the Heard Museum

Two weeks ago, we arrived in Phoenix, hot and tired from our two-day drive out from Dallas. But we were so excited, because March 4th, Friday evening, the Heard Museum hosted the Artist Reception and Dinner, and we were able to get a sneak preview of the award winning pieces and chat with some of the artists.

This is the 58th year that the Heard Museum has held their Indian Market, and they and their dedicated volunteers work hard to provide a quality venue for the Native American artists to display and sell their arts. The competition for ribbons is fierce, and the juries for each category often find themselves seeking the smallest details to help separate first place from second place. Even getting into the Indian Market is challenging, as artists must apply (with photos representative of their work) and go through a blind evaluation before they are even accepted to exhibit.

So Friday night was very special for Michael and me. We went into the Exhibit rooms, where they had both a Silent Auction going on, as well as a nice buffet dinner for guests. The highlight of the night, however, was moving into the two rooms that held the award winning pieces. Docents with white gloves were standing by each of the tables and insuring that nothing was disturbed, as these were exquisite pieces of art. As with other competitions, the categories were diverse, including paintings, pottery, textiles, sculpture, beadwork, jewelry, and many others.

While going through the pottery section, I signaled to Michael to come over to a table where I was standing. I asked him to identify the potters who had created the items, and without hesitation he immediately said that the first one was Dominique Toya and the second was Nancy Youngblood. They had both won First Place ribbons for their pottery entries, which came as no surprise to either of us. A Cherokee potter, Karin Walkingstick, also won a First Place ribbon for an unusually textured of pot. Cliff Fragua won two ribbons

Katie with Franklin Peters, Acoma master potter, doing a demo at the Heard Museum, circa 2016.

for his sculptures, and Meagan Shetima won a ribbon in the Youth carver category. It seemed that almost everywhere we turned, we saw a name of an artist that we knew (and usually had one or more of their pieces in our Gallery).

So Saturday and Sunday were full days at the Indian Market for us. We had to divide the roughly 600 artists into two parts, with a short list of people we wanted to see on each day. Then we set out to chat and visit with our friends. What is nice about this type of event is that even if an artist doesn't win a ribbon, their works are still very high quality and very collectible, so almost everything we saw was impressive.

Another part of the Heard Indian Market that we really enjoyed was the cultural activities, highlighted by the Zuni Olla Maiden Dancers and the Oklahoma Fancy Dancers. These groups performed each day and the comfortable grass amphitheater was an amazing venue for their dances. It gave us a needed break from all the walking, and we always enjoy the colorful regalia as well as the dancers telling us a bit about their dances, regalia, and traditions.

Another year of the Heard Indian Market has passed by, and the artists are already actively working toward the next venue, where they will once again engage in friendly competition for ribbons and bragging rights, as well as market their wares. For many artists, particularly those not represented in many retail outlets, this is their

Dance demonstration, Heard Museum, circa 2016.

primary source of income. We always encourage people who enjoy the look of Native American art to buy directly from the artist whenever possible, or through reputable galleries when you can't be at a show. This gives you the opportunity to learn more about the artist and gives deeper and richer meaning to the art itself.

The Santa Fe Indian Market is the largest show, held the third weekend of August each year. There are other venues as well, and we will try to spotlight those as they come up. If you get a chance, spend a day or two at a show and talk with some artists. It will definitely be time well spent.

What is Heishi and How is it Made?

The literal meaning of heishi is "shell" and specifically refers to pieces of shell which have been drilled and ground into beads and then strung into necklaces. More and more frequently, however, heishi (pronounced hee-shee) has come to refer to hand-made tiny beads made of any natural material.

The origin of heishi is fascinating indeed, and is inescapably linked to the ancient history of the people most proficient in its making, the Santo Domingo Kewa Pueblo and San Felipe Pueblo Native Americans. It is safe to say that this is the oldest form of jewelry in New Mexico (and perhaps in North America), pre-dating the introduction of metals. Centuries ago, the shells used by the Pueblo Indians to make beads were obtained in trade from the Gulf of California.

When one looks at a string of heishi, the first reaction is frequently "how on earth can a person do that?" or "to be so perfect, it must be done by machines." The truth is, if it seems exquisitely perfect, it was most likely made by the hands of a highly-skilled, extremely patient craftsperson.

Raw turquoise stones.

Knowing the steps involved in the creation of a good string of heishi can help a potential buyer distinguish—and appreciate the difference—between excellent hand-made jewelry and imitations. First, the raw materials are chosen. The most commonly used are seashells of all kinds—dark and light olive shells, spiny oysters, mother-of-pearl, and melon shell. Coral and stones such as lapis, turquoise, jet, pipestone and serpentine are also used to create exquisite contemporary heishi necklaces.

After the pieces are selected, now the process begins. With vulnerable fingers on either side of a whirring blade, the raw material is sliced into strips. Next, small squares are made by biting off pieces of the slice with a hand tool such as a nipper. Using tweezers to hold the tiny squares and a dentist's carbide bur, a small hole is drilled into the center of each square. After these rough squares of shell or stone are strung together on fine wire, the process of grinding, shaping and smoothing is begun.

The artist shapes the string of rough beads by moving the string again and again against a turning stone wheel, controlling the fineness and the diameter of the beads with his hands. At this point, many beads (stone or shell) will be lost - they will chip or will crack and fly off as the grinder catches a flaw or burr. Each type of material must be ground separately.

For example, pipestone and jet (high grade anthracite coal) are soft and grind down much faster than the harder materials such as turquoise, shell or lapis. Also, some materials are more difficult to work than others. With natural turquoise, for example, approximately 60-70 percent is lost. To minimize loss, each bead must be nipped into a rough circle before being ground. By now a string of cylinders, often graduated in size, has been formed and is ready for sanding.

The heishi is further shaped and smoothed with ever-finer grades of sand paper. The string is then washed with clear water and put in the sun to air dry. Finally, the string of heishi is given a high polish on a turning leather belt. The smooth, polished beads are now ready to be strung, either together or with other beads, as a piece of fine jewelry.

It will take anywhere from a couple of days to more than two weeks to make a single strand of heishi.

What to look for in a strand of good heishi - a string of good heishi will have a uniform consistency. If you gently pull it through your hand, it should feel like a single serpent-like piece. (Note: Precisely because of the handwork involved, a fine string of heishi may contain a slightly flawed or chipped individual bead.)

On the other hand, inferior "heishi-style" beads will often have holes that are too large, making the strand look and feel uneven and irregular. To make matters worse, this beadwork is frequently made of a variety of plastic materials of all colors, including block or reconstituted jet, coral or turquoise.

In the end, the quality of fine heishi comes directly from the ingenuity and integrity of the individual artisan. Learning something about the artisan, whether he or she has been reviewed by SWAIA for acceptance into Indian Market, or is a member of the IACA- Indian Arts and Crafts Association, are means of assuring that you are buying quality heishi. And of course, an ethical gallery or dealer will help you learn about the artist, the beads themselves and the creative process. The final guarantee is a certificate of authenticity which may be—and should be—requested from the individual dealer or gallery.

Different styles of heishi necklaces.

Adapted from: www.collectorsguide.com

Memories of Past Santa Fe Indian Markets

This weekend is Santa Fe's Indian Market, where the best of the best Native American artists gather to compete for prizes, display their creative talents, and share their traditions and cultures with the world. Indian Market is one of, if not the, premier showcase of Native American art throughout the world.

My mother and father always loved to travel to Santa Fe and dive into the flurry of activities during Indian Market. After a while, when they retired, they bought a small garden home in Santa Fe so they could spend more time with their Native American artist friends.

One story that Mom loved to tell was about her friends Ivan and Rita Lewis. They were from the Cochiti pueblo, and were quite well known for their storytellers. But, as is so typical with talented artists, it was not the only area of their work. Ivan briefly engaged in making pottery, and I am pleased to have the first bowl that he ever made. My brother, Jamie, has another pot that Ivan made, and with it the ribbon that Ivan won with that pot at Indian Market. My sister Maggie has a lovely large nacimiento set that Rita and Ivan made, as they both moved into executing characters. I also have three of Rita's storytellers, and they are exquisite. Recently I was able to add one more of Rita's storytellers to the Gallery.

But the core of the story is the relationship that Mom and Dad had with Ivan and Rita. Over the years, they got to know the other family quite well, and Mom and Dad counted Ivan and Rita as among their very best friends. One day, about a week before Indian Market, Mom got a knock on the door of their very tiny garden house. Did I mention how tiny it was? Mom went to the door, and it was Ivan and Rita. They cheerfully greeted Mom, and announced that they were here for Indian Market. So of course Mom invited them in, and they happily stayed with Mom and Dad through the completion of Indian Market activities. Over the years, Mom and Dad made a point of spending lots of time with them before Indian Market began.

And that is how their relationship went over the years. Drop by, say hello, maybe stay for a while, and build great memories.

Sadly, all great things must eventually come to an end, and a few years later Mom and Dad were honored to be invited to Rita's funeral, where the family followed Native American tradition and smashed one of Rita's best pots on her grave. A few years later, Mom followed Rita to the hereafter, and Dad did exactly what Mom had asked him to do – smash one of her best pots on Mom's grave, honoring the Native American traditions she loved so much.

Ivan Lewis bowl with award ribbon, circa 1980s.

I think of Mom's story every time I sit in my office and look at the Ivan and Rita Lewis storytellers. It isn't about the shaping of the clay, or the careful strokes of paint. It is about the years of time that Mom and Dad had with their wonderful friends. As I prepare to wade through the crowds at this year's Indian Market, I think I will have Ivan and Rita perched on one shoulder, and Mom and Dad perched on the other. And of course, Michael following behind with the bags of my new treasures. We will be visiting many of our Native American artist friends during Indian Market, renewing old ties and forging new ones. And I am sure I will have lots of fun stories to write when I get back.

Halona Inn at The Zuni Pueblo

If you ever make it south of Gallup to the Zuni pueblo, there is but one place to spend the night. Literally, there is only one place. It is the very historic and quite quaint Halona Inn, located in the heart of the Zuni pueblo.

The Zuni pueblo is one of the oldest continually occupied pueblos in the United States, having been started roughly a thousand years ago. Today, the thick pueblo walls and dirt roads evoke images of life back then, before electricity, automobiles, or most of the modern conveniences that we enjoy today. The Zuni pueblo, however, steeped in the ancestral traditions, still has no electricity or municipal water, and the residents embrace the lifestyle of their revered forefathers.

The Halona Inn was established in the 1880's as a trading post with the Zuni pueblo. The two homes next to the original trading post, built in the 1890's and 1910's, have been modernized and turned into a two-building bed and breakfast. These were the original homes of the trading post owners, and many artifacts and decorations in the bed and breakfast stretch back to the start of the trading post. There are only eight rooms, each decorated uniquely with Native American art.

The Inn at Halona, Zuni Pueblo.

Outside decks and courtyards, a nice little koi pond, and lots of seating on the patio – all the ingredients for a relaxing, restful stay in Zuni. The Inn was refurbished in 2013, and the beds are comfortable with spotless linens.

Avila and Anderson Peynetsa, Zuni potters, with Katie at the Halona Inn.

The true story of the Halona Inn, however, is not the actual buildings. It is in the personal attention and amazing service provided by Roger Thomas and his team. A Frenchman by birth, Roger has been in residence at the Inn since 1974, and he and his late wife spent countless hours making this Inn seem more like a comfortable home for guests rather than a typical bland hotel. A stocked kitchen in each building offers beverages and munchies for the late night snack attack, and breakfast is lovingly prepared to order from a fairly extensive list of options.

So the next time you find yourself in western New Mexico, wander down to Zuni (about an hour south of Gallup) and explore the Zuni Pueblo and meet some of the wonderfully friendly Zuni residents. We were delighted on our last visit when renowned potters Anderson and Avila Peynetsa dropped by. If you do decide to spend the night, make sure you have a reservation at the Halona Inn and say hello to Roger for me. We can't wait to return!

The Robert Nichols Gallery

Another stop worth making in Santa Fe is the Robert Nichols Gallery, located at 419 Canyon Road. I had the chance to stop in and visit with Robert recently, and he has a remarkable selection of both traditional and contemporary potters that he represents.

While chatting with Robert, I learned that he relocated to New Mexico in 1976 from Alaska, and opened his gallery in 1980. His background was as a research archeologist and curator for the National Park Service, giving him excellent training for becoming a gallery owner.

He managed to turn his interest in Native American art into both an avocation and a business, and has been happily adding to his collection ever since. Robert searches for new and innovative artists, such as Zuni potter Alan E. Lasiloo, and does a very nice job of telling their stories and supporting their endeavors. His focus tends to be on pottery, though he also has some photography and paintings in his gallery as well.

Robert Nichols.

So, yes, I did acquire a wonderful pot by Alan E. Lasiloo, and even though my tastes tend to run to the traditional pottery styles, I found this white clay pot with sheep tallow streaking in the glaze to be quite remarkable. It almost reminds one of the puffy white clouds hovering over the New Mexico landscape, hinting at the summer monsoon rains that renew life below.

Pot by Alan E. Lasiloo with sheep fat glazing.

Robert has recently added Mert Kenyon to his gallery staff, and Mert has brought another level of energy and vitality to the gallery. We had a chance to have coffee with Mert on a recent trip, and found his enthusiasm for his new home (he had recently relocated from the East coast) to be refreshing and quite delightful. Mert has dived in with both feet, and is rapidly becoming immersed in both the art and the culture of Native Americans in the American Southwest.

*Fences and walls keep people out, and keep people in.
But they always divide.*

IFAM's Second Year

IFAM is the Indigenous Fine Art Market, and is held in Santa Fe right before Indian Market. We had a chance to visit IFAM's Santa Fe show this year, in its second year of existence. The market featured about 250 Native American artists, and was held at the Santa Fe Railyard.

IFAM is more than just one show, however. The organization has much the same goals as other Native American art associations – to present and honor the culture, art, and traditions of the Native American peoples. To do this, they sponsor a number of pop-up events throughout the Southwest.

Though not as structured as SWAIA's Indian Market, IFAM has a low-intensity and soothing quality to it. We were fortunate to find parking at the north end of the Railyard area, and wander south among the linear layout of booths. There were a few people we wanted to see at IFAM, including fabulous potter Stacey Carr of Laguna Pueblo, fetish carver Gabe Sice of Zuni Pueblo, and amazing photographer Deborah Lujan of Taos Pueblo.

As with Indian Market, artists can submit their works for a juried competition prior to the start of IFAM, and ribbons are awarded. In fact, it is almost impossible to talk about IFAM without comparison to SWAIA's Indian Market, as the structures and goals are very similar. There are long lead times to apply to SWAIA's Indian Market, and some artists get too busy to apply, or forget, or don't want to spend the money on high booth fees, or for one reason or another decide to sit out Indian Market. Some choose to go with the gentler, less crowded approach of IFAM. The good news – the appreciation and demand for Native American art is so good that one single show like SWAIA's Indian Market is not enough, and IFAM is filling a needed void.

IFAM Opening Ceremony, circa 2015.

IFAM is talking about a pop-up market in Tulsa in the near future – I hope to drive up and see it, and connect with old friends and maybe make a few new ones. Tulsa has a lot more of the Plains Indians influences, whereas New Mexico and Arizona have more of the Puebloan and Mesa Indians influences, so perhaps we will see additional examples of Native American art that are of interest.

Emerging Artists at Indian Market

Every year, over a thousand extremely talented artists are accepted to show their creations at Santa Fe's Indian Market. The competition to get accepted is fierce, and many very talented artists are unable to participate. The ones who are selected to participate are the best of the best.

Every year, the entrants are a combination of established artists and emerging artists. Some of the established ones either retire or decide not to participate anymore, but the lifeblood of Indian Market is replenished with the new artists. It is always exciting to see our old friends, but also quite exciting to stop in and see some of the newer faces and get to know their stories as well.

This year, we had a chance to meet some new artists (a couple we had met previously, but they were fairly new to Indian Market). A Cherokee potter, Karin Walkingstick, caught our eye as we wandered through Market on the first morning. Karin was bubbling with excitement as we chatted on that crisp August morning, as she has entered Indian Market for the first time, and come away with a highly sought award ribbon for her entered pot. What makes this even more astounding is that Karin, though she has been working in different artistic media for many years, had only embraced pottery a couple of years ago. Her talent in making contemporary pottery is evident, as she has earned a number of awards in the past couple of years. Yet Karin remains humble about her craft and talent, deflecting attention away from herself and toward the pottery.

Another artist who was entering Indian Market for the first time was Deborah Lujan of Taos Pueblo. Debbie is a remarkable photographer, and she captures life at the Taos Pueblo with an amazing eye for composition and colors. Her lens tells many stories about the Taos Pueblo, including capturing for posterity some of the structures which are no longer there. All of her photos are shot with natural lighting, and there is no post-production altering of colors or shapes. What you see in her photos are incredibly beautiful vistas and icons of pueblo life. Debbie also won a ribbon at Indian Market, and we are so pleased to have several of her beautiful pieces in our Gallery. You can also see more about Debbie on her Facebook page, facebook.com/whiteflowerphotography.

Artistic talent may come from a source deep inside the soul, but it helps to have talented family members to teach and guide young artists. We had a chance to talk with an established and quite talented potter and silversmith, Erik Fender, and saw an item that his grandson Talyn (who was just 5 at the time) had done just prior to Indian Market.

In fact, it was Talyn's first ever piece, which proud grandfather had captured on Facebook, so we were able to acquire a piece of future history – the emergence of what will surely be another talented member of the Fender family. We were also able to purchase a piece by Erik's son, Ian. Ian is also developing his pottery skills quite nicely.

Ian Fender, San Ildefonso potter, 2015.

Oh, and did we mention that Erik earned a first place ribbon (of course) and an honorable mention ribbon, and his mother, Martha Appleleaf, and his son, Ian, also won second place ribbons. The talent runs deep in this family. And yes, we happily have a number of their works in the Gallery you can see.

Finally, a pair of potters who we had met at a prior show were also at Indian Market, and of course we had to stop by and collect a pot they had made for us, as well as chat a bit. Bobby Silas of Hopi and Tim Edaakie of Zuni have teamed up for a number of years to recreate the ancient and traditional design in their stunning pottery.

We saw Tim and Bobby earlier this year at the Zuni show in Flagstaff, but we were overloaded and couldn't carry another pot home with us. So we asked them to hold it for us, so we could pick it up at Indian Market. Being the perfectionists that they both are, they decided to create a whole new pot for us, fixing a couple of the almost impossible to see blemishes on the first pot.

Bobby makes the pots, and Tim does the painting, and this collaboration has won awards at Indian Market and at other venues. Both very talented in their own right, this teamwork often produces art that is greater than the sum of the parts. We are so happy to have several pieces of their work in our Gallery.

Bobby Silas, Katie, and Tim Edaakie at Santa Fe Indian Market.

So when you look at Native American art, look to the established names to get a feel for the best of the best. But also take a look at some of the new and emerging artists to see if they might have something that touches you. Even more than that, spend some time and talk with the artists and learn their stories. The piece of art then takes on a life of its own – created with the spirit of the artist, but also now linked to you. You'll never forget those moments, and your appreciation for the talent of these Native American artists will deepen each time you gaze at their craft.

Indian Market Reflections

Another wonderful Indian Market has come and gone. As Michael and I were sitting back reflecting on our trip to Santa Fe, we remarked on the many different points of view one could have regarding Indian Market.

For the first time visitors, of which there were quite a few, Indian Market is a wild, frenetic sea of tents and Native American artists, all showing authentic Native American art. It was quite interesting to see the different pueblos and tribes represented, as Native American artists see Indian Market as similar to the Super Bowl of their craft. It is where the best of the best Native American artists gather, and the first-time visitors marvel at the artistry of the weavings, pottery, beadwork, jewelry, paintings, and other artistic expressions. After a very short period, sensory overload takes place, aided no doubt by the 7,000 foot altitude of Santa Fe. Park benches are rapidly occupied, as shady respites are sought. There are dances in the street intersections, often small Native American children in full regalia showing their mastery of the buffalo dance, the eagle dance, or others. And everywhere one looks, there are people proudly wearing their best turquoise jewelry.

For veteran visitors to Indian Market, there is a bit of a different vibe. Certain artists are sought, and deliberate planning of visits takes place. This is what my parents did thirty or forty years ago – they found the artists they really liked and stopped to visit, and sometimes to buy. For this year's Indian Market, Michael and I had a short list of artists that we absolutely had to see, as we had built relationships with them over the years. We organized our list by street, and started looking for our friends. It is a really special feeling when an artist recognizes me, and gives me a big hug.

There is a small subset of the veteran visitors, the collectors. These are the folks who come to market with a mission. Often the mission starts on the Friday before Indian Market, when the SWAIA preview is held. The winners in each artistic category are announced, and ribbons are handed out to the artists. As the artists are not allowed to sell their wares prior to 7:00 a.m. on Saturday, the collectors take note of the artists and their booth numbers, and often line up outside the artist's booths before dawn on Saturday to get that winning piece of art.

Another small subset of the veteran visitors are gallery owners. We spent some time on Thursday afternoon visiting with several of them on Canyon Road, including Al Anthony of Adobe Gallery, Mark Sublette of Medicine Man Gallery, and Lyn Fox of Lyn A. Fox Fine Pueblo Pottery. Many of the galleries host artists during Indian Week, showcasing their works and giving folks a chance to meet the artists in person. These gallery owners are really special people, not only knowledgeable about Native American art, but also passionate about the art and support of Native American artists. They are honest and fair, and I am happy to count them as among my friends.

SWAIA, the Southwestern Association for Indian Arts, is the group that manages Indian Market, and conducts the peer judging of entries. They provide two ribbons – one for the artist and a duplicate ribbon that accompanies the winning art. The judging is an incredibly difficult task, as often the difference between first place and second place is a very minute bobble or brush stroke.

In addition to a continual effort to promote Native American arts, SWAIA does a wonderful job of organizing Indian Market activities each year. Indian Week is a weeklong celebration of American Indian culture, with dances, a lovely fashion show, and other different events leading up to Indian Market weekend. One event that Michael and I attended, as SWAIA members, is the Friday preview showing all the winning artwork. We also enjoyed the Saturday morning welcoming breakfast at Cathedral Art Park, with a wonderful live flute and drum duo setting the mood. Another event is the Saturday night Silent Auction, in which the artists donate incredible pieces of art for auction, with the proceeds going back to benefit the Native American communities.

Finally, the artists also have a perspective on Indian Market. Over 1,100 artists were selected for this year's event, with many of the best coming year after year to the same treasured locations. The streets surrounding the Santa Fe Plaza are closed on Thursday, and large canvas tents are erected beginning on Friday. Everyone has the same tent appearance, and artists spend Friday setting up their individual areas. Early on Saturday morning, before the sun peeks out of the mountains, they are setting up their wares and looking forward to two very long days of selling their wares. Many artists are electronically capable, taking credit cards or PayPal. Some take checks, and some take only cash. There are a few ATM's at banks on the Plaza, but those tend to run out fairly quickly - so be prepared. For many of these artists, this is their biggest weekend of the year, and we chatted with a number of artists who do very few events each year, so much of their annual income is derived from Indian Market.

So what are my major conclusions from this year's Indian Market? The event is very well organized, and SWAIA and the City of Santa Fe are to be congratulated and thanked for doing such a wonderful job. The atmosphere of Indian Market and the electricity running through all the tents and streets is amazing, because this event does an incredible job of celebrating the talent and skills of a very large, very diverse group of Native Americans. But even more important to me than acquiring more art (and yes, I did do a bit of that as well), is the opportunity to talk with the artists and learn their stories, to learn more about their culture and background, and to appreciate even

Eagle Dance performance, Santa Fe Indian Market, 2015.

more the dedication to their art that they have. Knowing an artist gives so much more meaning to their work. I sit in my Gallery in the quiet morning hours, looking at the new treasures just acquired, and I reflect back on the conversations I had with each artist. The sharing of stories, the growth of new knowledge, and the transfer of an artistic vision to a tangible piece of art – those are priceless memories that I bring back from Indian Market, and I will spend the next few months relating different tales from this year's market, and planning our next adventures to the American Southwest.

Museums – Curators of Culture

Museums are everywhere in our communities. I thought a lot about that on our recent trip through Arizona, New Mexico, Oklahoma, and Texas, as we visited a number of wonderful museums and reflected on others we have recently visited.

Museums started a couple of thousand years ago, as European communities began to accumulate surpluses of wealth, and used those surpluses either for religious or decorative purposes. Governments, religious organizations, and even prosperous businesspeople collected pieces of art that went beyond utilitarian, daily usage. In many cases, famous artisans were invited to live with the monarchs and wealthy businessmen, producing amazing works for both their patrons and for other purchasers.

The collections grew, and in some communities there arose dedicated structures to house and display these collections. In some cases, the collections were embedded into the community, and in other cases they were isolated and carefully preserved. Throughout Rome, for example, one can see fountains and statues created several hundred years ago by the government and the Roman Catholic Church. The artwork found in the Vatican is breathtaking, focusing on a narrow element of western culture.

Museums strive to gather the "best of the best" for their collections. A piece of art that is labeled "museum-quality" has a recognition that it is among the best of its type. Artists constantly strive to produce the best that they are able, and for the gifted and very talented the recognition of skill is bestowed by museum acquisition.

And the spread of museums has moved worldwide. It is estimate that over half a million museums of all types and sizes are currently operating in the world. They range from the very large, such as the Smithsonian in Washington D.C., the Louvre in Paris, and the British Museum in London, to small and very local museums such as the wonderful Copper Museum in Clarkdale, Arizona.

Museum of Indian Arts and Culture, Santa Fe, NM.

The purposes of museums are centered on conserving history and providing education to new generations. Both purposes are important, as the items and stories contained in museums helps carry culture from one generation to the next. Knowing our ancestral past, whether a hundred years, a thousand years, or even ten thousand years in the past, helps give each of us perspective, and gives us guideposts toward an unknowable and uncertain future.

The Native Americans carry forward their culture through storytelling. They tell stories with song, dance, regalia, pictographs, petroglyphs, and other means to celebrate their rich heritage, teaching their young the beliefs, values, and attitudes that form the culture specific to each tribe and pueblo. This is a vital function for the continuation of culture. Museums are the European attempt at storytelling, displaying art and giving narrative descriptions of the circumstances around that art.

The very best museums bring the stories alive, as we recently saw with the Indian Market at the Heard Museum in Phoenix. They hosted two days of Native American artists and their works, demonstrations, cultural ceremonies, music, food, and celebration of Native American art. This annual event fits wonderfully with the Heard Museum's mission, as they tell the stories of the Native Americans and the cultural disruptions and sometimes devastation brought about by their interface with European (new American) culture.

We have seen similar successes at museums like the Museum of Northern Arizona in Flagstaff, hosting a two day Zuni Carver market, the Museum of Indian Arts and Culture in Santa Fe, and the Indian Pueblo Cultural Center in Albuquerque. Each of these museums tells a part of the story of the southwestern Native American peoples, adding threads to that rich tapestry.

The Heard Museum, Phoenix, AZ

Every time I visit one of these museums, I learn more about the daily lives of Native Americans. Some are famous artists like Lucy Lewis and Margaret Tafoya, but many are just ordinary people like me. I learn more of how they interacted with sometimes harsh natural surroundings, struggling to find water and to grow crops. I learn more of how they lived in daily harmony with Mother Nature, carefully taking what they needed for life and honoring Mother Nature for the blessings they received. I learn more of their family live, and how important the extended family is to the Native American culture. And yes, I learn more of the dramatic changes brought about to their culture as it collided with the new American culture from Europe, rarely beneficial to the Native Americans.

Museum of Northern Arizona, Flagstaff.

But above all, I have learned to understand the Native Americans as individuals, people with dreams, hopes, struggles, and daily lives. I have had a chance to glimpse the world from their perspective. Above all, I have had a chance to build friendships with many people throughout the Southwest, talking, laughing, sharing stories and meals, and becoming a part of each other's lives. Some are artists, and I marvel at their level of skill, and some are ordinary Native Americans traveling the journey of life. I treasure each and every one of them, and I appreciate the role of museums for giving me a basic educations and rough understanding of the background and history of these proud peoples.

Indian Pueblo Cultural Center – A Story of Cooperation

The Indian Pueblo Cultural Center (IPCC) is located in Albuquerque, just off of I-40. Michael and I are members, though we only get to IPCC once or twice a year. We think the story of IPCC is important, and wanted to share a bit of it with you.

Just over 40 years ago, the 19 New Mexico pueblos got together and decided that they needed an objective, professional way to share the rich history of the pueblo peoples with the rest of the world. In 1976, they opened the IPCC, showcasing not only the story of the pueblo peoples, but also the amazing artistry that has been developed over the centuries by these people.

IPCC carefully and respectfully tells the story of the pueblo peoples, tracing the evolution of the pueblos from the ancestral Native Americans through major paradigm shifts like the arrival of the Spanish conquistadores, and the challenges of preserving Native American culture and belief systems while also living in the Anglo world. The exhibits are very professional, and the contributions of artifacts are rich and stunning to examine.

Unlike many museums, IPCC is constantly alive with interactive events and activities. They feature authentic, traditional dances, often bringing in dance groups on the weekends from not only the pueblos, but also Native American tribes from around North America. The pageantry, colors, and music are always informative and captivating to watch.

In addition to showcasing historic and current artists, IPCC seriously embraces its role as an educator, hosting frequent talks from experts on subjects as wide ranging as water conservation to traditional pottery making. Fortunately, many of their talks are recorded and available on the IPCC website, and I always seem to learn many new things when I watch the videos.

Numerous events are scheduled every month - there is always something wonderful and informative happening at IPCC. For the month of March one of the events is a "Celebration of the Legacy of Lucy Lewis" and how it is carried on by her family and students.

Another upcoming event during this month as a continuation of *Women as the Creators and Keepers of Tradition* is a view into the IPCC collection of Pablita Velarde, Helen Hardin, and Margarete Bagshaw. Make plans to visit the incredible center and continue to learn more about the pueblos, their history, and their wonderful people.

There are two other things that really make IPCC a wonderful tourist stop for both families and tour groups alike. The first is the Pueblo Harvest Café, where Executive Chef David Ruiz and his staff prepare delicious menus. They often have special features, such as their upcoming Valentine's Day Dinner, and give us an opportunity to really explore pueblo foods done well.

The second, which is also among my favorite aspects of IPCC, is Shumakolowa Native Arts. This exquisite outlet for Native American works is simply packed with Native American treasures at all price points. Not only authentic pottery, textiles, jewelry, paintings, and other pueblo art, but also books, music, clothing, and wonderful treasures for all pocketbooks.

Ask Manager Ira Wilson or anyone on his team about an item, and they can tell you the back story and help you to be a more educated buyer of authentic Native American items. Ira goes out often to buy the items directly from the artists, and he has lovely blogs and lots of photos that really convey the hard work that these artists put into their craft.

IPCC just opened a huge Starbucks as part of their operation, and I can't wait to see this newest addition. This year, IPCC celebrates its 40th anniversary, and they have a lot of special birthday celebrations planned to mark this wonderful milestone. Stop by and check it out, or if you have been in the past, stop by and see what is new. I know it is well worth your time!

Once again, we will be visiting there soon. And I can't wait.

Katie outside the Indian Pueblo Cultural Center (IPCC), Albuquerque.

A Lucy Lewis Retrospective

What an amazing weekend we just had at Shumakolowa. Ira Wilson, who heads the gift shop, arranged another spectacular event, and we were able to bend our schedule just enough to participate. Ira had the daughters and granddaughter of Lucy Lewis give a panel presentation and tell stories about Lucy, and it was truly memorable.

Lucy Lewis, Acoma Pueblo, Matriarch potter.

Ira, having been at Shumakolowa for the past 25 years, is well connected to the Native American communities of New Mexico and Arizona, and he arranges these events to preserve the stories and traditions of this vibrant culture. Over 150 people were enthralled by the stories about Lucy, as these stories are ones you can only get directly from family members.

Lucy's daughters Carmel, Delores, and Belle were on the panel, as well as two of her granddaughters. Delores, who traveled with her mother while growing up, also served as Lucy's interpreter for much of her appearances, as Lucy spoke mainly the language of her Acoma pueblo - Keresan. Delores told a number of great stories about some of the trips she and her mother took, such as the one to New York City where they went to see the Rockettes, and the trip to the Big Island of Hawaii, where Lucy fell in love with the beautiful flowers and weather. Through her career, Lucy traveled to many places, including a special trip to the White House in 1977.

Her granddaughter, Shayai, talked about how Lucy always used to wedge the clay with her feet. When asked, Lucy said she didn't know why she did it, so Shayai speculated that Lucy wanted to be closer to Mother Earth, which provided the clay for her use. Shayai also reminisced about growing up around the Lewis household, surrounded by numerous cousins. Lucy and her husband Toribio operated a working ranch, and raised nine children. The children stayed near the family home in adulthood, except for her oldest son Ivan, who went into the Marines during WWII and then married and relocated to the Cochiti pueblo with his wife Rita.

Acoma Polychrome Geometric Bowl, Lucy Lewis, circa 1980s.

The family spoke of a household that didn't have electricity for the longest time, and how they did their homework with kerosene lamps. They played in the arroyos around the home, and went out to collect the cow dung used in firing the pots. Of Lucy's nine children, seven went on to become potters, some gaining acclaim in their own right.

One of the most touching parts of the discussion about Lucy was when the discussion revolved around Lucy as a real person, not some iconic and untouchable figure. Lucy was warm and generous to everyone she met, and had a very caring personality. She met notable figures like Vincent Price, the Prince and Princess of Monaco (who came to a wedding at Jemez Pueblo), and many others, but always treated them just like normal people, much the way she wanted to be treated. Her family said that Lucy never knew that she was famous, or that the work she did at Acoma Pueblo influenced so many Native American potters, and that was just fine with Lucy.

At the end of the event, nobody wanted to leave. Everyone stayed to chat with the Lewis family, and I was so pleased to get to meet the daughter of Ivan and Rita Lewis, who were close friends of my own mother and father. I told them that I had Ivan's first pot, and it was a very precious part of my collection.

I also have a pot of Lucy's, one from her daughter Carmel, and another one that I managed to acquire from Ira this afternoon from Lucy's daughter, Emma. The pots are exquisite, and I have loved looking at them over the years, but now they are even more special to me because I have the memories of this very special event that the Indian Pueblo Cultural Center and Shumakolowa put on today, helping preserve the immense legacy of this wonderful potter, Lucy Lewis, and helping keep alive the memories of a real person who had an incredible talent.

Katie and Carmel Lewis, at IPCC, 2016.

Starbucks at the Indian Pueblo Cultural Center

Earlier this year, the Indian Pueblo Cultural Center (IPCC) in Albuquerque opened a large, modern Starbucks across the street from their facility. It is a great place to stop for coffee or a sandwich, and Michael and I have added it to our "go-to" stops while in Albuquerque. Of course, this is typically after I have downed an order of my favorite blue corn onion rings from the Harvest Café at IPCC.

I've written about IPCC before – how it was founded 40 years ago by the 19 New Mexico Pueblos, working together to showcase the culture and art of their peoples. In addition to the magnificent museum displays, they have an amazing museum shop (far too classy to call it a gift shop), frequent cultural exhibitions and dances, and significant presentations and meetings on topics relevant to Native Americans and other residents of the American Southwest. It is an absolute "always stop here" when we go through New Mexico, and I am really pleased with our memberships.

So, as they always do, the creative people at IPCC decided to do something both symbolic and fun with the opening of their new Starbucks. They went to a few noted Native American artists, including my friend Erik Fender, and asked them to create something which tied together the rich heritage of the Native Americans and the new coffee hangout. Erik came up with a tall coffee cup similar to a venti beverage cup, only in San Ildefonso black pottery and engraved with Native American symbols.

Erik says that the first try wasn't successful, as the pottery cracked during firing, and he had to try again. The next cup was successful, yet just a bit too large for the Starbucks plastic coffee lid. So he put that cup in the Than Povi store at the San Ildefonso pueblo, and tried yet a third time. The third time was the charm for Erik, as this effort produced just the right size cup for the Starbucks lid. This third cup is on display at the Starbucks store in Albuquerque, highlighting the elegant combination of traditional Native American pottery expertise with the Native American artwork throughout the store. There is some talk that the third cup may be the model for some replicas, and I think if Starbucks was smart they would jump all over that one.

Erik Fender's second IPCC prototype.

So what happened to the second cup that Erik made, the one that was successfully fired but not quite the right size? Yes, you are right! I managed to add that unique, one-of-a-kind creation by Erik Fender to my gallery, together with the silly white plastic Starbucks lid! No, we will never use it for any beverages – this precious piece of pottery is far too significant for that. It is a piece of pottery that is unusual, but also one with a great story behind it. Every time I look at it, I think of Erik's smile, of the lid that didn't quite fit (lucky for me that it didn't!), and the smart and creative folks running IPCC.

In a nutshell, that is the excitement and pleasure I have in learning the stories behind the magnificent art produced by the Native American artists of the American Southwest. While one can appreciate the beauty of the pottery, jewelry, carvings, paintings, textiles, and baskets, the story behind the art is the real treasure. That is what art is to me – the people, their lives and labors, their cultural influences, all providing rich context to the art that they create. It is all about the story.

Laguna Potter Stacey Carr

One of the true pleasures of having a gallery is the opportunity not only to have a collection of wonderful pieces of art, but to get to know some of the artists on a personal level. Earlier this year, I was able to visit with Stacey Carr, a wonderful Laguna potter. I had been talking with Stacey for a while about his work, so I asked him if it would be ok for us to drop in and meet him while we were driving from Zuni to Santa Fe. He graciously agreed, so we set out from Zuni on a crisp, beautiful spring morning on another adventure.

Michael and I followed Stacey's directions, and found his house without difficulty. He invited us in, and we had a chance to meet his lovely wife and son. After we chatted for a while, Stacey invited us into his studio, where he makes and paints his work.

Katie and Stacey Carr, circa 2014.

As with many Native American potters, Stacey gathers his own clay from the hills surrounding the Laguna pueblo, and builds his pots with a pinch method instead of the more traditional coiled method. What I found fascinating was the amount of time that Stacey spends on detailed painting of his pots, exhibiting amazing patience and delicacy. As with most outside-fired pottery, there are times when Stacey fires a batch of pots and finds broken ones from the irregular firing, so those which are completed are amazing works of art. He has won a number of awards at the Heard Museum, Indian Market, and many other venues.

Although most Laguna potters use the traditional Acoma grey clay mined in and around the pueblo, Stacey prefers to use the non-traditional red clay for his pottery. "It is much more challenging to work with, I like the deep intense color." He usually chooses to paint his red clay pottery with black paint (handmade from wild spinach) which creates a beautiful contrast against the red.

Stacey shared one of the reasons he like to make this beautiful, but difficult pottery. "The beauty is in the pottery itself. I love making it, and I love the art. It is art of the highest quality."

Detailed traditional pot by Stacey Carr, Laguna pueblo, circa 2014.

We found Stacey to be very outgoing and friendly, enthusiastic about his art, and eager to share his knowledge with others. He has done a number of videos on YouTube, sharing his techniques with aspiring potters. Stacey also volunteers his time by conducting demonstration workshops on pottery, trying to encourage others to learn the skills needed to be a successful artist. I learned a lot about pottery by listening to Stacey, and am happy to count him among my artist friends.

Stacey attended The University of New Mexico and majored in biology. He still lives in the Laguna area. He learned the art of pottery making from his ex-wife and her parents. It was from them he learned to find the clay which would make good pottery. He learned how to soak, grind, and knead the clay before ever beginning to create a piece of pottery. Today, he has emerged as one of the leading Native American potters, and continues to produce stunning works of art.

People of Action

I am writing this today on Red Nose Day, which is targeted at helping end hunger among children around the world. It is a meaningful effort, and one that Michael and I have supported with our own red noses.

But today is just one day. There are 364 more of them out there each year, and so many ways in which we can all make a difference. This blog is to celebrate the actions of several Native American artists who, in their own ways, make a big difference in the world. And I am very happy to have these people of action as my friends, partly because they are talented artists, but also because their hearts are so wonderful.

The first is Stacey Carr of Laguna Pueblo. Stacey is a talented potter who grew up in Old Laguna, and his roots run very deep in the community. Earlier this year, Stacey noticed that the basketball courts where he had played many years ago had fallen into disrepair, and he took action. Stacey organized a group of people who cleared off the debris and overgrowth from the courts, fixing items that were broken, and bringing this neglected facility back to life. He did it not for money or recognition, but because it was an important task to do for the children of the pueblo.

Basketball hoop repair, Laguna Pueblo.

The next is a cluster of artists – Maxine and Dominique Toya of Jemez Pueblo, Nancy Youngblood of Santa Clara Pueblo, and other family members – who spend countless hours traveling the country to demonstrate traditional Native American pottery skills. In doing so, they communicate far more than just their skills and techniques. They communicate their values, their culture, and help educate people about the stories of the Native Americans who form such an important piece of our heritage. Seeing the art through the eyes of the artist, and hearing the stories from the souls of the artists, makes this art more understandable and approachable. Their public service is invaluable.

Zuni Main Street Days flyer, 2014.

And then there is Jeff Shetima of Zuni Pueblo. There is a thriving community of fetish carvers and sculptors at Zuni, but it has been fragmented and underpublicized in the past. Jeff has taken a strong role in organizing Zuni Main Street Festival, a celebration and juried competition among Zuni carvers, and has worked tirelessly to help other carvers become better businesspeople to help showcase their spectacular talents.

Each of these artists does many other things as well. Some are active in SWAIA, the organizing group for the highly acclaimed Santa Fe Indian Market each August. Others work closely with their Pueblo governing and religious organizations. Some donate pieces of their art to auctions and fund-raisers for their communities. But what helps to set these very talented artists apart is that they are dedicating a part of their valuable time to helping others. They take the time, they make the effort, and they work to help others because it is the right thing to do. At the end of the day, actions speak far more than words, and these people of action quietly deliver.

I guess that makes me a member of their fan clubs. I know how hard it is to create magnificent pieces of art, to raise families, and to handle the daily grind of life. That these wonderful people make the time and effort to help others in the ways they do just leaves me in awe and heartfelt appreciation.

Artists are far more than just their art. The more that I am among them, in their homes and studios, hearing their stories, sharing meals with them, and just hanging out, the more that I see the depth of their creativity and fall in love with their works.

Zuni Pueblo Kiva Expansion project.

Water

Water. I sit here this morning watching another dreary day of scudding clouds and seemingly endless rain. This is the second spring in a row that Texas has had enormous amounts of rain, followed by flooding and tragedy.

Water is a good thing. It is necessary for our survival. The surface of Mother Earth is over three-quarters covered by water, and our own bodies are more than sixty percent water. Without water, we do not live long.

But even as plentiful as water is on Mother Earth, it is mostly laden with salt. Only the fresh water that falls from the skies is useable by us. It falls as snow or rain, it collects in lakes and rivers, and then heads back into the vast oceans from where it originated.

As such, fresh water can be unpredictable. The low pressure system currently sitting over Texas has caused torrential rains and flash flooding, yet areas in California are still in long droughts. Rain falls where it wants, and when it wants. This is the natural cycle that has given life to the land, but on its own terms.

Native Americans have long been aware of the natural rhythms of Mother Earth, and recognize the value of rain as a gift. Some of the earliest Anglo stereotypes of Native American dances are "rain dances" in which the Native Americans are purportedly trying to summon rain. Fortunately, over the years, we have moved beyond those stereotypes and recognize that the Native American dances are a means of communicating with Mother Earth and her creatures, a means of expressing respect for the abundance of resources found around us, and a means of passing stories and traditions on to subsequent generations.

Thousands of years ago, as the First Americans began to move throughout the Southwest and form settlements, they recognized the sometimes erratic nature of fresh water. Rivers would flow, and the First Americans would plant crops and irrigate. Lakes would have teeming stocks of fish, and land animals would frequently travel to rivers and lakes for a drink of fresh water and sometimes an afternoon snack.

Sometimes, the heavens would pour water from the clouds, and parched desert canyons would turn in to raging floodwaters in almost a moment's notice.

Water Prayers, David Dawangyumptewa, Hopi artist.

At other times, the rivers would stop flowing and lakes would begin to dry up. These shifts in climate patterns forced the First Americans to abandon their settlements, like Casa Grande, Bandelier, and Chaco Canyon, and migrate to areas where fresh water was more abundant. This dynamic interaction of the First Americans and Mother Earth was a basis for the formation of their beliefs, attitudes, religions, and cultural practices. Every morning, my friend Samuel Manymules, a Navajo potter, greets the morning with blessings and thanks to Mother Earth.

Michael and I were recently honored by being asked to attend a sacred evening dance at a New Mexico Pueblo, at which the dancers – elegantly attired in traditional dance attire – paid tribute to the brave Comanche tribe with which they have interacted over the centuries. Often, at events like the Phoenix Heard Museum Indian Market or the Santa Fe Indian Market, Native American dancers perform ceremonial dances for throngs of appreciative visitors. Even better, they explain to Anglos some of the culture and significance of their dances.

The interaction of Native Americans with water, and with the other richness provided by Mother Earth, is both spiritually touching and increasingly relevant to all of us. The lessons of water and other natural resource conservation, learned through thousands of years of trial and error by the Native Americans, are important lessons for all of us to learn.

The typical Anglo approach to Mother Earth is to force the land to do our bidding, as we foolishly think that we can control the environment. But as resources dwindle and the population increases, we are starting to realize that we can't continue down this path of endless, mindless consumption. The Native Americans have lessons for us to learn. It is up to us to listen carefully and live in more harmony with the blessings of Mother Earth.

Colorado mountain stream, photo by Stacee McClain, circa 2015.

Repair and Restore

Life happens. No matter how carefully people try to take care of pottery, jewelry, weavings, paintings, and other pieces of art, life happens. Sometimes it happens because the pot or weaving was meant as daily use ware, or the jewelry was meant to be worn rather than just placed in a box on the shelf. At other times, it is because the piece is showing its age, and has accumulated scratches, nicks, or similar signs of wear.

So as lovers of Native American art, what do we do? One option is to ignore the wear, and accept the piece with its new imperfections. That is certainly a valid option. Another option is to have the art carefully restored by a professional, perhaps preserving the original beauty of the piece or fixing some of the damage. Again, it is a valid option.

If you choose the second option, I have a couple of suggestions. For pottery, we were referred to a wonderful man in Corrales, New Mexico by the name of Andy Goldschmidt (Ceramicare). Andy has been doing pottery and ceramic restoration for decades, and is well regarded among gallery owners and museum curators for his meticulous work. We decided to visit Andy last year, and see for ourselves. After a circuitous ride through Corrales, we finally drove up to Andy's studio.

Inside, we found Andy among shelves of damaged pots, some of which were quite large and historic. We chatted with him for a while, and found him to be quite pleasant and knowledgeable. I hesitantly left a matched pair of old Margaret Tafoya ollas with Andy, asking him to repair a rim chip on one and a scuff chip on another. Andy gave us an estimate of cost and time, and said that they would be ready in about 6 to 8 weeks. When they arrived at our gallery, they were extremely well packed and looked magnificent. Only with the use of a black light could you see where he did his delicate work. His charge was just what he estimated, so we happily sent off a check that same day.

Another recommendation is in the area of jewelry. The Navajo, Hopi, and even Zuni jewelry artists are wonderful, both in their silversmithing and in their use of precious and semi-precious gems. But sometimes a necklace breaks, or a prong needs fixing, or a stone needs to be replaced.

I had been reading great things about Dayton Simmons of Madrid, New Mexico, (silverdaytrading.com) and we made a special point of stopping to see him at this year's Indian Market. He is a fascinating man with an

Katie discussing turquoise with Dayton Simmons, expert gemologist.

endless store of knowledge about turquoise, a stone highly prized and heavily utilized by Native American artists. We chatted for over an hour, and he gave us a great tutorial on natural turquoise (his specialty) and stabilized or treated turquoise. We learned how to feel the texture and visually inspect the stones to determine whether or not they were natural.

I left several pieces with Dayton in a little baggie, including some of my mother's old turquoise earrings that I needed converted from screw back to posts, so I could more comfortably wear them. Dayton has quite an eye for age and quality, and gave me some very valuable feedback on the value of the items I was leaving, as well as several pieces I was wearing.

So a few days later, as we were heading from Santa Fe back to Albuquerque to catch a plane home, we detoured into the beautiful hills of eastern New Mexico to the sleepy community of Madrid, where Dayton has his shop. There used to be turquoise mines in New Mexico, but those have largely been exhausted. Dayton still enjoys tromping around in the hills seeking interesting rocks and possibly even some undiscovered turquoise. His studio is part museum and part retail shop, with a number of interesting exhibits of different types of rocks.

As a gallery owner, I have found that it is important to have a healthy network of quality Native American artists, but equally as important to have a strong network of trustworthy experts who can provide knowledge and even assistance with preserving the rich heritage of Native American art. I am happy that Andy and Dayton are two such experts, and even more happy with the friendships that we have built with them.

Everyone has the ability to change.

Not everyone has the will to change.

Rugged and Beautiful

The land of the American Southwest contains vivid contrasts in appearance. Many millions of years ago, what we now know as Arizona, Utah, Colorado, and New Mexico was close to the equator, and part of a large inland sea. Continental drift moved this land north and tectonic pressures caused massive uplifts in the land, resulting in the Rocky Mountain chain and the high plains of the Southwest. Volcanos were quite active as well, and much of New Mexico and eastern Arizona remain covered in thick layers of extruded lava. Relentless wind and water also helped shape much of the terrain, exposing colorful layers of sedimentary rock and fossils, eroding steep bluffs, and carving meandering canyons.

An initial impression of the American Southwest is one of raw, harsh, and almost forbidding terrain. Much of the land is high altitude, over 5000 feet, and vegetation struggles to gain a hold in the parched soil. Sources of water are at a premium, and many of the early Americans settled in areas where water flowed consistently. In many cases, when the water ceased, the communities also moved to other areas where water was more prevalent.

But when one looks longer and deeper, one sees a surprising palette of colors and shapes. One of my friends, Brian Yatsattie, posts pictures of sunrises and sunsets that are rich and vibrant natural portraits. Michael and I recently traveled through Sedona, with highway turnouts every few hundred yards so we could park and admire the red and tan horizontally striped mesas. In eastern Arizona, we drove through the Painted Desert, a National Park Service treasure with amazingly beautiful exposed canyon walls.

Sedona, AZ.

In addition to the physical structure of the land, Mother Earth has added her gentle touches to the American Southwest. As one drives south through Arizona, the high plains grasses give away to stands of saguaro cactus on the craggy peaks, or large stands of pine trees. The saguaro are magnificent, some living to over 150 years in age. Their beautiful, delicate white flower is the State flower of Arizona. One can often see bird holes carved in the sides of the saguaros, providing safe nests for woodpeckers, wrens, martins, and a variety of other avian desert dwellers.

We also went through Payson, a charming town in the midst of the largest Ponderosa Pine forest in the world. The flora has adapted to the altitude and climate, conserving the scarce water deep within their structures and sending deep tap roots into the earth. Some plants secrete chemicals that help break down the lava and rock into dirt, and anywhere a crack appears through erosion or other processes, plant seeds soon attempt to gain a toehold. That is, of course, if plants had toes.

Similarly, the fauna has adapted to the conditions. Energy conservation strategies are prevalent, ranging from rough skins and camouflage colors to cool burrows and remarkable endurance. During the day, you won't see much moving about, as most animals gather food during the very early morning or late evening hour when the temperatures are more moderate. As we explored a little of the magnificent countryside, we saw lots of creepy crawlies, many that sting or bite. Snakes, spiders, scorpions, and similar critters that we left alone, and asked them nicely to leave us alone as well.

When the early Americans arrived in the Southwest, they saw much of the beauty around them, and also found ways to adapt to the local conditions. They saw the advantages of constructing safe rock dwellings along the cliffs, using or constructing caves and homes. They were very aware of the scarcity of resources, and utilized what they had very carefully. Many of the traditions honoring Mother Earth came from those early interactions and utilizations of the scarce resources. Rather than using the European approach of changing the earth to fit the needs of individuals, the early Americans adapted their ways to live in harmony with Mother Earth, a gentler and more economical approach.

Almost everywhere we go in this world, we can see the natural beauty inherent in the land. The American Southwest presents a type of beauty that is very different from that found in Europe or the eastern part of the United States. It is raw, primal, harsh, colorful, vibrant, and yes, quite alive.

Outside Sedona, AZ.

Enoch Kelly Haney, Seminole/Creek Statesman and Leader

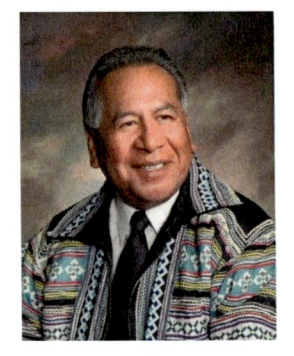

Kelly Haney is, in my humble opinion, a sterling example of a Native American treasure. In November of this year, he will celebrate his 75th birthday. Hopefully Michael and I will be able to travel to Oklahoma City and drop in on his gallery to give him our birthday wishes.

Kelly is a full-blooded Seminole, and in 1980 was elected to serve in the Oklahoma Senate as the first full-blooded Native American to serve in either house of the Oklahoma legislature. After serving in the legislature for six years, Kelly ran for Oklahoma Governor in 2002. Kelly has been a tribal councilman, and from 2005-2009 served as the principal chief of the Seminole Nation of Oklahoma. But political service was only one of Kelly's many careers.

Enoch Kelly Haney, Seminole/Creek artist and statesman.

As a Master Artist, Kelly has painted many acrylic, oil, and watercolor paintings. One of my favorites, Flute Player. is shown after the book's title page. Kelly draws inspiration from his proud Seminole heritage, particularly portraying family members. In the Flute Player, it is believed that the subject is Kelly's father, Woodrow Haney, who was a renowned Native American flute carver and player in his own right. In fact, I am fortunate to have one of Woodrow's handmade bird flutes and a signed cassette tape of his music. Kelly's paintings are vibrant in their natural color schemes, detailed in capturing the essence of Seminole people, and emotional at a very deep level. In 1976, the Five Civilized Tribes Museum named Kelly as a Master Artist.

But that isn't all for this amazing man. On top of the Oklahoma State Capitol building is a 22-foot tall bronze statue, "The Guardian," done by Kelly and erected in 2002. He has a number of additional significant bronze sculptures located in governmental buildings and high-end galleries throughout Oklahoma. Stop by the Chickasaw Nation Headquarter building in Ada, Oklahoma and you'll see his "Chickasaw Warrior" bronze.

Being a productive member of society comes in many different ways. Some people are fortunate to have an artistic talent. Some people are leaders and visionaries. Some people educate and nurture others. There are lots of other ways. What I love and respect about Kelly Haney so much is that he has accomplished so much in all of these many ways, and has helped the people of the Seminole Nation with his efforts. And in doing so, Kelly has also helped all of us. That is the mark of a treasure – one who inspires others through his or her deeds and actions.

Kelly Haney, photo taken from an old sales brochure.

A Simple Piece of Silver

As a small girl, I accompanied my parents on many, many trips to the American Southwest. Though many of my earlier memories are somewhat vague due to the darkening shroud of time, one stands out with crystal clarity.

Mom and Dad would take me, and later on my younger siblings as well, on wonderful road trips through New Mexico, Arizona, Colorado, and Utah, exploring and learning about the different groups of indigenous peoples who lived there thousands of years ago. I remember climbing through some of the cliff dwellings at Mesa Verde, and walking all about at Chaco Canyon.

Those experiences were great, but my favorite memories are when I got a chance to meet Native American artists and talk with them. That was so much better, in my young opinion, than seeing some old monuments and rocks. I got to hear their voices, see their clothing, and learn to appreciate them as people just like me, but with a different cultural background.

And it was on one of those trips, when I was only about 7 or 8 years of age that one of my earliest, most vivid experiences was created. Mom and I were walking down the portico of the Palace of the Governors, where Native American artists set up their displays and show their wares. I don't remember if Dad was walking behind, or if it was just the two of us that afternoon. I think I had my entire life savings in my little purse, but there really wasn't anything being shown that really caught my interest. I was just having a grand time stopping and admiring, and hearing my mother talk with some of the artists that she knew.

Suddenly, the light caught a silver object near the front of one of the blankets, and it called out to me. It was a simple silver pony-tail holder, and at that point in my life, I was all about pony-tails. I remember looking at it, and then asking my mom if I could pick it up and look at it. I think she knew right away that it was going home with me, so she and the artist both smiled and watched me examine the lovely silver art from all different angles. After careful consideration, I dug into my small purse and pulled out enough money for the pony-tail holder. I don't know if mom helped out or if the artist gave me a break, or both, but somehow I had enough money for the piece. As I grew up, I proudly wore that piece for years, until the time came that I was out of the pony-tail stage and into young woman hairstyles.

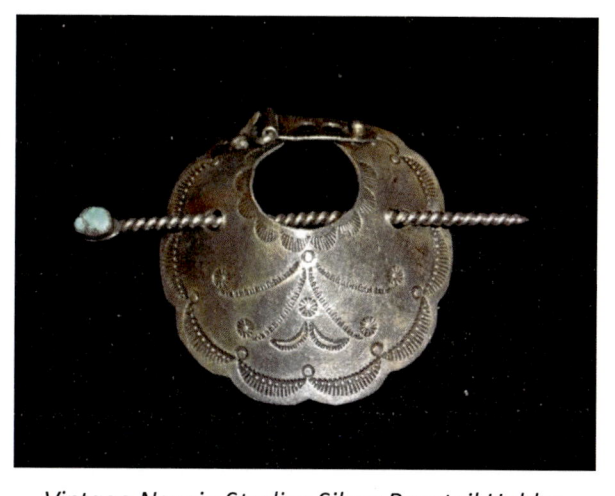

Vintage Navajo Sterling Silver Ponytail Holder, artist unknown, circa 1960.

But I kept the piece, as it was one of my earliest memories of Native American art and meeting and learning from Native American artists. Clearly, it is not one of my most valuable pieces, but some things can't be measured in money alone. To me, the memories of getting the pony-tail holder are priceless, because that simple piece of silver helped launch me on a life-long journey of learning about the peoples of the American Southwest and their legacy of art.

Quirky Jerome, Arizona

A couple of hours north of Phoenix, and quite a ways off the Interstate, you will come across the quirky little town of Jerome. The town is perched on the edge of a volcanic caldera, and the houses are often cantilevered out from the side of the steep mountain. A narrow road snakes through town, with rough driveway sized side roads leading to some of the private residences.

It is almost 150 years old, and owes its initial growth to a large deposit of copper that was mined a century ago. Originally discovered by early Americans and mined for surface deposits of azurite and malachite, the copper deposits became some of the richest deposits found in the world. Within a period of about 70 years, over 33 million tons of ore were mined. A few miles down the road, in Clarkdale, the Copper Museum displays the history of copper and all the historic and modern uses of it. Today, Jerome is a small community of artists, coffee shops, a few retail stores, and the Grand Hotel.

The Grand Hotel has a fascinating history, as it is an outstanding example of buildings constructed during the roaring 20's. Initially built as a hospital, it was closed in 1950 and subsequently reopened in 1994 as the Grand Hotel. The manual self-service Otis Elevator was the first in Arizona, and it is a lot of fun to open the outer door, then the inner door, and enter. Repeat the process, select one of the floors in this five story building, and reverse the process to exit the elevator. The Asylum Restaurant on the second floor is open for lunch and dinner and has really great window views along with a superb butternut squash soup.

Jerome Grand Hotel.

The Grand Hotel, and much of Jerome, has a reputation for being haunted. Some attribute the haunting to Claude Harvey, the maintenance man who was found deceased below the elevator in 1935, allegedly murdered. Crying babies and other apparitions are also heard and seen in the hotel, giving it a reputation among those seeking supernatural thrills.

Following the copper mine closure in the early 1950's, Jerome subsided into a struggling, almost deserted town. Over time, a small artist colony formed, with artists attracted to the scenic views (and unoccupied homes) in Jerome. Today, the Jerome Historic District (almost the entire downtown area) consists of small galleries and retail shops, interspersed with a few restaurants and other service businesses. One of our favorite places to eat is Haunted Hamburger, which goes all out to promote the haunted town image. They have good burgers, too.

So if you are driving between Phoenix and Flagstaff and want to get off the beaten track for a bit and explore some of the history of Arizona, head to Jerome. Drive slowly, as the roads are narrow and winding. And you never know when you might get the urge to stop, take some pictures of the panoramic Verde Valley, marvel at the homes and garages precariously cantilevered out over open space, or visit with a local artist.

It's Just a Rock …
Guest Story by Jamie McClain

I acquired a somewhat large piece Turquoise some time back. Not really sure why I wanted one, because I carry a small one in my pocket. I tell folks it's for good luck. Truth is I just like carrying it. This one is much too large to carry, so it sits on a shelf with some treasures I have acquired over time.

The other day I was asked why I had such a pretty rock among my little carvings. Well that opened a door that I had to just run through. I explained the history around the "carvings" fetishes, that they were prized possessions and traded or bartered among the carvers, and sometimes were believed to bring certain things to owners such as good luck or even divine advantages.

The pretty rock was in fact Kingman Turquoise native to New Mexico, and was from which some of the Navajo, Zuni, and Hopi Native Americans made their jewelry. Of course I had to show off a Squash Blossom Necklace that my wife has. I tried to explain how the silver and turquoise process took place to make the jewelry, of which my knowledge is very limited. After a long conversation regarding such things and discussing some of my pottery and baskets, my mind began to wander some.

Turquoise from various Southwestern United States mines.

As the holiday season approached and Christmas was closing in, I began to see the "pretty rock" as a work in process; much like people are. We all have good qualities; we all have something inside of us waiting to be finished. If the artist never used the piece of turquoise it remains just a "pretty rock." On the other hand when the artist begins to work with the stone and chip away the "undesirable" parts. Then works it into the shape desired, polishes it, and places it in a setting, it becomes much more than a pretty rock or an unfinished turquoise stone.

As we think about Christmas true meaning, and how a simple event changed the world forever. And the opportunity given to us to chip away our undesirable pieces; I remember that seemingly insignificant pretty rock. It, was we do, have the ability to become much more when the "Artist" works it into a beautiful piece of jewelry. Admired by those who see much more than a pretty rock.

Adios for now, Jamie.

Joe Hayes and Tortilla Flats
Guest Story by Jamie McClain

Story telling is an art form used to share culture, traditions and fond memories; it can even be used to teach a lesson or two. New Mexico's favorite storyteller is Joe Hayes. For children and adults alike, his storytelling sessions outside the tepee at the Wheelwright Museum in Santa Fe are a summer tradition that has continued for over 35 years. Joe's tales are a combination of the traditional lore of the American Southwest and his own imagination. During a few of our family trips to Santa Fe, my mother treated her grandchildren with an opportunity to listen to Joe Hayes share his enthralling stories and to read his books. My brother Jamie shared just one such family memory with me recently:

It was a visit to Santa Fe that would impact my kids and me for the rest of our lives...

My mother had made plans for a day of "literary experiences" for my two boys, who at the time were around 4 and 6 years old. Being a school teacher, my mother planned days which meant either going to a museum or a cultural center for an educational experience. With young children in tow, I was all too cautious that she would expect us "boys" to be still and pay attention. To say I was a good influence in times such as these might be considered a stretch of the imagination.

So the next morning we were awakened to energy and excitement that would rival any Christmas morning, as far as my mother was concerned. As the day progressed, my mother's excitement grew; it was late in the afternoon before it was finally time to leave. We drove for a while and arrived at the Wheelwright Museum. I sure nailed that one.

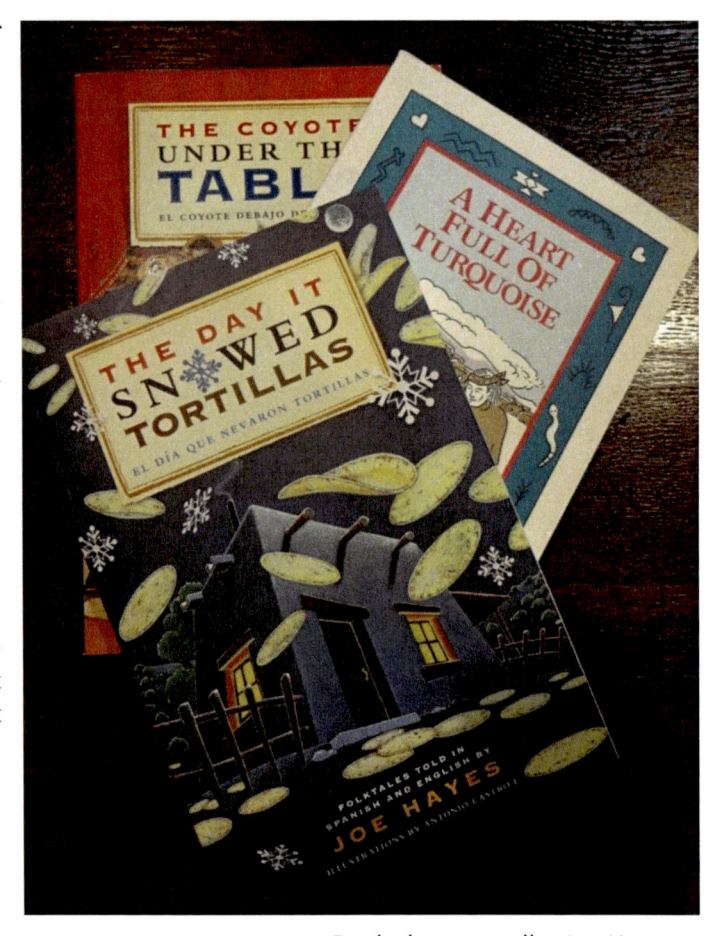

Books by storyteller Joe Hayes.

There was a hum of excitement as people walked around, many heading to a secluded area found only by an earthen path way. As we approached the area, we could see a tepee with a fire pit to one side of it, which projected a feel of a very relaxed atmosphere. Large logs provided seating in front of the tepee.

We took our places and Mother promptly excused herself and strolled toward a man standing to one side. He had somewhat long hair, glasses, and was wearing a white shirt and blue jeans. She hugged him and visited for just a few seconds before returning to sit with her grandsons.

As the sun set and dusk crept in, this plain dressed man walked to the front of the audience and silence fell over the crowd. He introduced himself as Joe Hayes. I almost fell off the log I was sitting on. I had read some of his books to my kids; he was a famous southwest storyteller and author. Now I understood my mother's excitement. Joe Hayes told enchanting stories and spun yarns that made you feel as if you were part of the tale. My sons were as motionless as I was as he shared his story of "The Day It Snowed Tortillas." As the flames of the fire began to die down and the evening came to a close, I went over and hugged my mother, and she smiled and put her hands on my face and glowed. As if hearing Joe Hayes in person wasn't enough for all of us, Mom stopped and introduced the boys to him. A wonderful and gracious man, Joe even signed a couple of books that my mother had purchased earlier and he told us a quick story of his childhood. What an evening! I am not sure who was more excited - my sons, my mother, or me.

My sons are grown now, but from time to time we recall the evening that "JoJo", their grandmother, gave us all something special to remember and to share through the ages - a great memory to cherish. Thanks, Mom.

Adios for now, Jamie.

Wisdom is knowing enough to ask questions.

Biscohitos - A Family Christmas Tradition
Guest Story by Jamie McClain

As a youngster growing up, I saw our Christmas decorations as an eclectic mixture of traditional Christmas with a big dose of Santa Fe and Taos thrown in. We had strings of chili peppers around the Christmas tree in the den, decorated with little pots and basket ornaments; red chili ristas hung by front door; and luminaries lining the drive, helping visitors easily find our house. Navajo rugs were on the floors and two large katsina dolls stood on each end on the fire place hearth.

One of my most cherished memories was the baking of biscochito cookies. Whether you call them biscochitos (northern New Mexico) or biscochos (southern New Mexico), these cookies are just simple short bread cookies sprinkled with cinnamon and sugar - but their taste is quite unforgettable. There are several variations of this recipe, but the flavors are the same - cinnamon, sugar and anise.

These delightful little cookies are the official State cookie of New Mexico - which is the only State to have an official cookie. In fact, during the 1989 State legislative section, battles erupted over the correct spelling of this wonderful delicacy introduced to the area by Spanish conquistadors back in the 17th century. Quite a history, indeed!

As an annual Christmas tradition Mom would make biscochitos by the dozens - and there were never enough, as far as I was concerned. They were revered and savored by folks who came to call during the holiday season. Special friends might even end up with a small box of them to take home on their departure.

Mom would always cut some into special shapes for me - cowboy hats, cowboy boots, and even cactus shapes. Texas stars and the small round shapes were always popular. She even had a special "cookie tin" to keep them in. These southwest cookies, to say the least, were at the top of the Christmas goodies list at our house.

Traditions are special to each and every family, and ours is not any different. After Mom passed away, it was a few years before I got biscochitos freshly baked without a visit to Santa Fe or Taos. Now my sister, Katie, has rekindled this tradition of heavenly goodness by baking biscochitos every year using Mom's recipe. So visits between our homes during the holidays mean two things to me:

Biscochitos in various shapes – always tasty!

happy times to reminisce of family and Christmases past, and a cookie tin of biscochitos just for me. Of course I share with my amazing wife, but you can bet the count is carefully monitored.

I hope for you this Christmas is filled with family traditions that rekindle joyous memories, and blessings beyond measure in the coming year. Feliz Navidad! Jamie.

Slumgullion Pass and Historical Markers
Guest Story by Jamie McClain

My mom and dad were the type of parents who believed that a historical marker was to be read and shared. With that said, I most likely can tell you the gist of almost every historical marker between Fort Worth, Texas and Lake City, Colorado. From famous settlements to trails blazed by Kit Carson, cattle trails and Indian raids, and any happenings that made an impact on early life as the movement west was in full swing, these are the historic events my family stopped to read and learn about as we traveled. Historical markers along the roads to Taos Pueblo, the Santa Fe area, and Los Alamos are some that specifically come to mind.

I believe once we even stopped to read about the oldest pecan tree in Texas. I'm sure Lady Bird Johnson would have been disappointed in the fact all I wanted to do was climb it—as a young boy, couldn't have cared less how old it was.

Although I really didn't like stopping to read ALL of the historical markers along our summer travels, there was one that I eagerly looked forward to every summer. As the family camper headed north out of Santa Fe, we traveled toward Colorado and my favorite marker. As we came over Slumgullion Pass and headed down into Lake City, my folks would always stop at the Alfred Packer massacre site.

To me history never had a more interesting marker. Mr. Packer and five other prospectors became lost, and snowed in just outside of Lake City Colorado. By today's standards it couldn't be more than a few miles out, but in 1873 it might as well have been a thousand miles, under several feet of snow and temperatures that would freeze the skin in minutes if exposed. Survival for these over-confident souls would take some devious thinking.

History records that Mr. Packer did just that. To survive he consumed the other prospectors. At a young age of 8 to 11 years old, to me that was real history. And as I was told many times, historical markers are as factual as books in school.

As the years come and go, I recall many of the places I have been, but none remain as memorable as the Packer Massacre site. In next few weeks I will return to the Ouray, Lake City area of Colorado. You can bet if time allows, the jeep will trek over Engineer's Pass into Lake City and straight to the huge bolder with the bronze plaque on it to read once again.

Bon Appétit until next time, Jamie.

Slumgullion Pass Historical Marker.

Boredom Becomes Stardom - Briefly
Guest Story by Jamie McClain

Later in my "at home" years (I believe I had to be 17 if memory serves me correctly), my parents and I again left Santa Fe headed to Lake City, Colorado. My sisters had left home for college or had married; family vacations were something from which they had an exemption. For me, vacations were something I looked forward to - fly fishing, jeeping in the high country, and even going to dances at the lodge were exciting.

I didn't need a date at these dances, as there were lots of girls there on vacation with their folks. So a dance partner was as close as the next table - and a tall handsome, rodeo cowboy with hat and trophy buckle to match was in high demand at these dances. Or maybe they just felt sorry for me, either way I was golden. And if needed, I could always dance with my cousins who joined us in Lake City each summer. So saving face was always at hand.

One day, my aunt and uncle, along with my folks, went to Gunnison for the day. And as luck would have it, my father deemed it necessary to NOT leave me the keys to the truck. So after hanging around the R.V. Park for as long as I could stand it, I had a great idea. I would go to the stables out toward Lake San Cristobal and rent a horse and trail ride for the day.

So I stuck out my thumb (very grown up), and hitched a ride toward the lake. I was let off just outside of the gate, so my walk was not very long. After procuring a horse with saddle that both fit my level of riding and ego, I started off on my individual adventure. The trail I was instructed to ride followed the Lake Fork of the Gunnison River- a somewhat mundane trail I thought. Being around horses, rodeoing and cowboying I thought I needed a diversion from the well-traveled path.

Jamie McClain, bronc buster and roper.

As time passed, I found myself crossing the Henson Creek Bridge. I took a left and headed toward town... to say I was noticed is an under-statement. My adventure had somehow turned into a one man parade. As I rode down Main toward the one and only drug store to have a root beer, a lady approached me and asked several questions - my name, where I was from, and so forth, and she took my picture. Well, time passed pleasantly as I rode until finally I had to return my rented mount. I'm sure Roy Rogers never felt the way I did that afternoon. I was the hero (of something) and everybody waved as I rode by.

After my family returned from the day trip, I was asked if I had seen the "cowboy" who rode his horse through town. How they knew of the event I couldn't figure out. My mother would ask this only as she knew of my love for horses. The next day we were scheduled to leave, so packing was our focus for the evening and nothing more was said of the cowboy riding through town. Next morning we said our goodbyes and headed home.

Dad stopped to fuel up before we left Lake City, and I went in to pay. There on the counter was the local paper with a picture and story of a cowboy on horseback in front of the Drug Store. I almost swallowed my tongue. I wasn't supposed to ride except along designated trails, much less in town. And I wasn't supposed to leave the R.V. Park or the vicinity of Henson Creek, within reason. I felt like Billy the Kid as I left the gas station at a high lope, sure someone would recognize me and block my get-away. Seems in less than a matter of hours, I felt like I went from hero (of something) to outlaw in sleepy little Hinsdale County. Well, we made it out of town without indecent. The Hinsdale County Sheriff never showed up at the county line with a warrant, and none of my folk's friends mailed the article home as a memento.

History repeated its-self the next summer as we again went from Santa Fe to Lake City. Thankfully the imagined wanted posters and the newspaper article were long forgotten and once again we enjoyed the high country that is Colorado.

"Happy Trails" - Jamie

Every argument has two sides.
The truth is often somewhere in the middle.

The Old "58"
Guest Story by Jamie McClain

When I was a kid, my father purchased a 1958 Ford F100 pickup from my grandfather (his father).

Now this was in the late 60's so factory air, cruise control, and other standard equipment that we take for granted today were not even considered on a pick-up. Along with the pick-up, he purchased a cab over camper - again no A/C, potty or shower were available. The shower was a large wash tub and a water bucket used during our tent camping adventures - long before the big "up-grade" to the camper. The truck had a three-on-the-tree shifter, a hot water six cylinder engine, and a top speed of a blazing 57 mph. Remember; this was an up-grade!

Stopping on the side of the road, somewhere in New Mexico, to view the scenery.

Every summer we would load the rig up and head to Colorado, via Santa Fe, for some "culture experiences;" my mother was a school teacher, so every trip had to be educational. And my father would say "being well rounded never hurt anyone." But being the youngest, while crammed into a camper with two sisters who wanted to stay home anyway, I found these educational experiences, well, could be a little painful.

We would arrive in Santa Fe, after what seemed like days of driving across Texas in the heat. Immediately we walked the square, going into every little gallery and visiting with the owners. I never knew two people could know so many people away from home as my parents did. We never took the main paths; the back alleys and shops that only the local artisans knew and used was our itinerary. It was more like a well plotted battle plan - as if someone was going to get the goods before us.

Dad would negotiate on the rugs, pottery, baskets, and turquoise jewelry while creating a friendship that would last the years. I always found it interesting that Christmas cards would come from several of their friends from the region. Because of their persistence in educating me and exposing me to this culture, I came to respect and enjoy the Native People of New Mexico along with their magnificent works of art.

1958 Ford F100 Pickup with camper – like we used to have.

Years later Mom and Dad started the *Dancing Rabbit Gallery* to share their love of all things Native American. After my parents passed, my sister, Katie and, her husband, Michael, rekindled the gallery with support from my sister, Maggie, and myself. The legacy and the education will continue now, although not as painful now, but with lots memories and laughter.

Oh, and the 58? It went back to my grandfather a few years later, and I got it when I turned 16. Wish I had it now...

Adios for now, Jamie (the little brother).

When I Met Charlie Eagleplume
Guest Story by Jamie McClain

One vacation I remember was to Rocky Mountain National Park. As a side trip we went to a trading post near Estes Park, and all I remember was Mother's excitement of getting there.

I was pretty young, so I don't recall much of the trip with exception of the "really cool stuff" that was there. As instructed by my folks, I had my hands in the pockets of my jeans. "I could look with my eyes, not my hands," they told me. I think my poor sisters were in charge of keeping me out of trouble during our visit - I'm sure that was a full time job.

As time passed, there was an elderly man in a rocking chair talking and visiting with those who had entered the post. While pestering my father to purchase something for me, and him trying to explain that the "really cool stuff" wasn't for little boys, he motioned to Mom and escorted me toward the elderly man. As I was introduced to "Charlie Eagleplume," his voice and gentle manner of speaking mesmerized me.

Charlie Eagleplume, circa 1960s.

He spoke of things that he had done as a little boy and how poor he was. After a time he asked, "what do you think is the most important thing that you can have is?"
> Was it money?
> Was it friends?
> Was it toys?

He leaned forward, and gently took my hand (at this time I'm sure I was spell bound) and whispered "Love is the most important thing you can have..."

He then took out a box full of arrow heads and allowed me to choose one. I put my new treasure in my pocket and cherished it for years. Although through the years I lost the arrow head, the truth remains today. Love is much better than the "real cool stuff." Seems today we could use a lot more love for one another, and a little less of the cool stuff.

Adios for now - Jamie.

Window Rock, Arizona – Navajo Nation Home

The Navajo Nation is the largest sovereign Native American nation in the United States. Yes, it is under Federal jurisdiction, but it operates as a separate country within its far-reaching geography.

The center of the Navajo Nation, or Tségháhoodzání in Navajo, is the small town of Window Rock. With under 3000 people, it is a typical small town in America, with all the fast food, convenience stores, and other typical things one would expect. But they have one additional facet – the Navajo governmental offices. The Navajo Nation President and Vice President, the Navajo Nation Supreme Court, and many of the supporting governmental offices are located right at the base of the stunning Window Rock landmark.

In March, Michael and I had a chance to drive through Window Rock, and we stopped at the Navajo Nation offices. The Navajo Nation Museum is located there, as well as the Navajo Nation Zoo. The Museum offers wonderful insights into the culture and ceremonies of the Navajo peoples, and provides a rich tapestry of the art and artifacts of this proud people.

If you want to get some original Navajo art, you have several outstanding choices. The Hubbell Trading Post is located outside Window Rock, and is run by the National Park Service. Inside this historic site, there are quite a few rugs and other pieces of Navajo art available. The best, in my opinion, are those of the very talented Two Grey Hills weavers, though Ganado, Chinle, and Wide Ruins are also amazing in their complexity and quality.

Another option, located in Window Rock, is the Ch'ihootso Indian Market Place. You can find a wide variety of art, including stunning Navajo sterling silver jewelry, each day at this market. The Zuni, located a couple of hours southeast, and the Hopi, located a couple of hours to the west, also come to the market from time to time.

Window Rock, heart of the Navajo Nation.

But the most interesting thing we saw in Window Rock was the weather-sculpted redstone rock itself. The Navajo refer to this as a mystical place, and their governmental offices are built at its base.

Window Rock, Bronze honoring Navajo Code Talkers of WWII.

The Navajo have erected a Veteran's Memorial at Window Rock, including a stirring bronze of the many Navajo soldiers who served, and are currently serving, in the United States armed forces. The most famous are the Code Talkers, who provided not only an unbreakable tactical code but also risked their lives as U.S. Marine artillery spotters in the fiercely fought Pacific theater during World War II.

Michael and I had a chance, last year, to visit with the last of the original Navajo Code Talkers, Chester Nez, before he passed away earlier this year. The Navajo are making sure that their Veterans are receiving the proper honor and recognition that they are due.

So if you ever find yourself wandering across Arizona or New Mexico on I-40, and you are near the eastern border of Arizona, take a side trip for a few hours up to the tiny city of Window Rock. The deeper you dig into the stories and culture of the Navajo peoples, the more impressed you will be. The rock, as a geological formation, is nice to observe. The history of the Navajo people is fascinating and well worth the time in the Museum. But the true benefit will come from connecting with the culture of an existing, vibrant, proud people who are successfully combining their ancient traditions with the realities of the modern world. As much as Plymouth Rock or the Golden Gate Bridge, the Navajo are a part of the American story, and comprise a rich chapter that deserves respect and appreciation.

Success is often preceded by hard work.

Meeting Samuel Manymules, Navajo Potter Extraordinaire

We often think of the Navajo people as outstanding weavers, as evidenced by the textiles that come from areas like Two Grey Hills, Ganado, Chinle, and others. We also often think of the Navajo people as amazing silversmiths, learning their trade from the Spanish explorers and traders in the early 19th century, and improving on those skills through the centuries.

But, as are most groups of Native Americans, there is considerable diversity of talent behind the common stereotypes. I have found a number of excellent Navajo potters, such as Alice Cling and Samuel Manymules, over the years.

Imagine my excitement at Indian Market this past August, when I got to meet Samuel Manymules and chat with him for a while. He only goes to Indian Market and one or two other events each year, preferring to stay at his home in the four corners region, close to the center of the sprawling Navajo Nation lands. So when I saw his name on the artist list this year, I circled it and made a point of stopping to talk. As we stood on the veranda near his display, many people stopped and admired his work, commenting on the swirling smoke clouds in the pottery created by the outside firing, and remarking on the shapes he creates.

Samuel (not to be confused with his son Sam) is a very spiritual man, as are most of the Native Americans who are very close to Mother Earth. Each morning, he goes outside to face the east and give thanks to the rising sun, seeking the blessings of the spirits and energizing his soul. When we finished chatting with Samuel, he spent a few minutes giving me a Navajo blessing - a memory I will always treasure.

"I build my pots first in my mind," says Samuel Manymules. In little over one short decade, the pots he envisions have made him the quintessential 21st century Navajo potter and winner of numerous Native American Arts most prestigious awards.

Samuel Manymules, Navajo potter, Santa Fe Indian Market 2015.

Born on the Navajo reservation of the Bitterwater Clan for the Red Horse Nakai Dine Clan, he grew up in the Navajo way: tending flocks, and working in the cornfields. Along the way he discovered ancient pottery sherds and became fascinated with their shapes and patterns. It is a fascination that lasts to this day. After dabbling in several jobs, including jewelry making, Samuel discovered that creating pottery was to be his avocation.

Long before he sets his hand to clay, Samuel sits and plans. "I spend most of my days envisioning the shapes, planning how to make the vision a reality, and imagining how the completed pot will look." Only then does he begin to work with the clay.

Using only traditional natural materials, Manymules transforms melon jars into swirling asymmetrical shapes; water jars into swooping, gravity-defying creations; and, into the immediately recognizable faceted pots for which he is renowned. He manipulates traditional shapes into precise architectural angles that only a master potter's hand could create.

Samuel Manymules unique approach to creating beautiful traditional pieces of art has placed him at the forefront of traditional Navajo pottery. He is one of the most highly collected Navajo potters today. His award winning work marks the continuing movement of Navajo pottery to more sophisticated forms with more refined finishes.

So yes, to complete the story, I did manage to limit myself to purchasing only two of Samuel's wonderful pots that day, but I am sure they won't be the last.

Which Squash Blossom Necklace Would You Choose?

Whether made by the Zuni, or the Navajo – or even someone from Taos, each of these necklaces is beautiful. The squash blossom necklace, since its creation in the late 1880s, remains an elegant and stunning work of art.

The squash blossom necklace, with its silver beads, as well as the naja crescent moon centerpiece, is remarkably unique. The flower pendant is actually a representation of the Spanish-Mexican pomegranate, but is commonly referred to as a squash blossom.

When the necklace with its crescent moon or naja came into existence, the Navajo people had been under the influence of Spanish Conquistadors for hundreds of years. The naja symbol eventually began to represent agriculture and was first used as a pendant on a simple cord. As the Navajo learned the art of silversmithing, they began to make silver beads - Navajo pearls - to string with the naja. The Navajo called the squash blossom bead "yo ne maze disya gi," which means "the beads that spread out."

Most squash blossom necklaces that can be found today were made during the 20th century, and retain the same sense of beauty of the original pieces. Turquoise and coral are most commonly inset with the silver beads and the naja pendant. No matter whether simple silver beads, or needlepoint turquoise, or larger chunks of turquoise or coral – each one is magnificent and should be worn often.

A Winters Chill

The Christmas trees are down, and all the decorations are put away for another year. Outside lights are also down, which means the electric bill can return to some measure of normalcy. The celebration of the New Year, with accompanying resolutions for self-improvement, are also in the rear-view mirror.

From around North America, reports are coming in of cold weather, snow, and dull gloomy days. The pictures of fresh snow glinting on the ground are pretty, as are the ones of falling snowflakes being tossed about in the wind. Ten degrees and four inches of snow in Zuni. Fifteen degrees and a foot of snow in high-altitude Santa Fe. Five degrees and two feet of snow in high-altitude Flagstaff. We don't even want to consider Minneapolis or Winnipeg – negative temperature reports send chills up my spine. Another wintry season settles in, as we all cross off the days until spring returns. We passed the winter solstice last month, and the days steadily grow longer and longer, but winter will still have its icy grip on us for weeks to come.

Yet, somehow, we survive this annual cycle of cold and warm. Snow and sunshine. The winter is the time when many artists work hard in their studios and homes, transforming raw clay into stunning pottery; putting pigments to canvas; molding silver into ornate jewelry. This is the season of preparing for the New Year, getting ready for upcoming exhibitions and fairs, and figuring out how to be successful when the weather changes back to uplifting warmth.

Yes, I admit it freely – I am a sunshine person. I adore the long days of bright sun, basking in its comforting rays. My garden plants grow, colorful flowers bloom, and the birds sing their happy songs. It seems to me that the whole world comes alive in the spring, awakening from its long, dreary winter slumber. On days like today, when we have limited sunshine, near freezing temperatures throughout the day, and a layer of ice on the birdbath, I huddle in my gallery beneath layers of clothes and even a blanket or two, shivering with the cold. Thick wooly socks fail to keep my feet warm, and there is no hope for ever getting my cold nose warm again – until the gentle caress of spring's warm breezes.

It is said that living in the Deep South thins the blood, and makes one less resistant to cold weather. I went to college in Oklahoma, and lived there for a few years afterwards, but I guess back then I was hardier. In the 90's, I moved to Colorado, and suffered through a couple of winters there. I returned to Texas to let my blood gracefully thin once again. I fully believe that saying about thin blood, and also believe that I am living proof of it.

For those living in the north (by which I mean everyone north of the Texas border), I tip my hat in appreciation of your abilities to survive in the winter. I know that you have winter activities, like strapping two pieces of wood to your feet and sliding down mountains, or cutting a hole in a frozen lake and waiting for fish to investigate. I admire that you are embracing your situation and finding satisfaction in these activities, and even sharing pictures and videos on Facebook and other social media. But, sadly, I must decline to partake of these activities on my own. I raise my cup of hot chocolate in salute to each of you, and cross another day of winter from my calendar.

Santa Fe – A Spectacular Place to Explore

Even as a small child, I have always had a special place in my heart for Santa Fe. My parents used to take us on vacation every summer, and no matter where we went, it seemed like we somehow went through Santa Fe for a bit of the vacation. When they retired, my parents even bought a tiny garden home in Santa Fe for extended summer trips. Conde Nast Traveler selected Santa Fe as one of the best small cities in the United States for tourism, and I completely agree.

The first thing a visitor notices about Santa Fe is the altitude. At 7,000 feet, it doesn't take long for the thin air to cause one to take a break and get a drink. Fortunately, there are many tourist-friendly spots where one can sit and rest for a minute. Because of the altitude, the weather is crisp in the summer mornings, and mild during the day.

Every visitor should start with a visit to the Santa Fe Plaza. This historic area has the Palace of the Governors, La Fonda Hotel, and dozens of small retail stores and restaurants. Many of the buildings are historic, with thick wood beams in the ceilings and plaster or adobe walls. On W. San Francisco St. we even found a wall plaque commemorating Billy the Kid, who apparently was as fond of Santa Fe as we are. La Fonda Hotel, in addition to being a nice place to stay (all the older rooms are uniquely decorated, though the new expansion has more standard hotel rooms), has a wonderful enclosed courtyard restaurant with tasty food and potent margaritas. Remember the altitude? That makes the alcohol even more potent, so be careful.

Breakfast at Tia Sophia's is a must. It is a small Mexican restaurant on W. San Francisco, just a couple of blocks off the Plaza, and has really good food for breakfast and lunch. Getting in can be a challenge, but they have a numbering system where they give you a card with a number written on it, and when they call your number, you are ready to eat. Wonderful people, excellent service, and a great experience.

Another breakfast option is Tecolote (owl in Spanish). They just moved to a larger place on St. Michael's Dr. and they have a very clean, modern interpretation of Mexican food for breakfast or lunch. Don't let the strip-mall location fool you – this is a really great place to eat.

If you want to eat where the locals eat, try the Tune-Up Café on Hickox St. Both indoor and patio (front porch) seating, and some tasty tidbits that will knock your socks off. Waffles that float off the plate, fabulous coffee, and much more.

Dinner is another opportunity to explore. We really like La Choza or The Shed for authentic Mexican food, Café Pasquale for more rustic Italian food, and La Casa Sena for incredible food, service, and atmosphere in the outside courtyard dining. The nice thing about Santa Fe is that there is a wealth of fine restaurants at all price points and with different styles of food, so everyone can experiment and find something to their liking.

Beyond restaurants, Santa Fe is loaded with museums and galleries, many featuring historic and contemporary Native American art. Some, like Andrea Fisher Gallery, are right on the Plaza, and others are located on nearby Canyon Road. Lyn A. Fox Fine Pueblo Pottery and Adobe Gallery, as well as Medicine Man Gallery and Robert Nichols are just a few of my favorite places to wander through, visit, and purchase wonderful pieces to take home.

Another place to begin exploring is the museum at the Palace of the Governors. Originally built by the Spanish in 1610, it has served as a government building for many years. Every weekend, Native American artists gather in their appointed spots to show their wares in the Portico of the Palace of the Governors. Many of these artist spots are handed down through the families.

An amazing landmark on the Plaza is the Saint Francis of Assisi Cathedral, which is about 150 years old. It is built in the French Romanesque style, and has lovingly tended grounds and inspiring interior sculpture.

Nearby is the Loretto Chapel, also about the same age as the Cathedral, but built by the Sisters of Loretto order. In the Chapel is the Miraculous Staircase, with legend attributing it to St. Joseph the Carpenter due to its 360 degree spiral and no nails!

St. Francis Cathedral, Santa Fe.

There are so many things to do in Santa Fe that it could take weeks for me to write about all of them. Michael and I have enjoyed our many trips to Santa Fe and will continue to share some of our adventures with you.

Standing Bear Powwow

Native American tribes gather in community celebrations called powwows. Typically they dance, hold contests, share information, and conduct the business of the tribe.

However, there is an unusual powwow called the Standing Bear Powwow, held every year on the last weekend of September in Ponca City, Oklahoma. It is unusual in that it is the center of six nearby American Indian tribes, who join together for a large intertribal powwow.

Standing Bear was a Ponca Native American chieftain (1829-1908) who was one of the first successful plaintiffs in US Courts working to improve the legal and social standing of Native Americans. Ponca City, Oklahoma, has dedicated a magnificent park to his memory, with a large statue and sacred dance arena. The Standing Bear Park is a 63 acre site, complete with a very educational Museum.

The six tribes are the Kaw, Osage, Tonkawa, Pawnee, Otoe-Missouria, and Ponca tribes. Each tribe brings a princess in traditional regalia, and the inter-tribal powwow princess is crowned. There are traditional tribal dances, competition dances, and singing and drumming. Of course, no powwow would be complete without storytelling and mingling of cultures.

Standing Bear opening blessing, Ponca City, OK.

The powwow has a variety of vendors, selling Native American items and foods. Typical of Native American hospitality, the six tribes invite everyone in attendance to join them in a Saturday evening meal of fruit, fry bread, and corn soup.

The Grand Entry is held twice, and dancers enter in full ceremonial regalia. It is a very casual event, with no admission charge. The event starts on Friday afternoon, and continues through Saturday night. Bring your own folding chairs, and get ready to enjoy a wonderful couple of days of learning and enjoying.

Standing Bear Powwow, Ponca City, OK.

Turquoise Inlaid Wood

It is a show stopper.

Several people have asked about the wood vases I have in the Gallery, generally because the turquoise inlay catches their eye. The ones I have are simply stunning. I acquired several of them from Clint Cross, a Native American artist living in Colorado. The Burtis Blue Mine, which is still running today producing beautiful natural turquoise in blues and greens with a soft brown matrix. Burtis Blue Turquoise comes from the oldest running family owned turquoise mine in the area around Cripple Creek, Colorado. All of the turquoise mined here is still dug by hand – the old fashioned way. This mine produces top quality gem grade turquoise. Clint carefully shapes his pieces and then inlays the tiny pieces of natural Burtis Blue turquoise that he has personally mined. The pieces are then given a hardening agent to keep them in the wood. They are increasingly finely sanded and sealed to achieve a smooth surface and preserve the natural hues of the woods and inlay.

Clint Cross, North Eastern Abenaki, turquoise inlay artist.

These pieces are beautiful, but very labor intensive to create. In addition to the hours of work to make the wood host and dig the turquoise, each step of the process often involves hours or even days of waiting time until the next step can be undertaken. As with other artists, Clint's creations become a labor of love, and his painstaking attention to detail and craftsmanship are evident when one sees or holds his work.

Examples of turquoise inlaid wood.

Turquoise inlaid wood pieces add the soul of the Southwest to any home décor. The natural movement and structure of the wood determines where to place the inlay chunks or large cabochons of turquoise. Many wood working artists use finely ground turquoise, which brings different shapes and hues of color to the bowls, vases, picture frames, or tables. Michael and I have seen dining room sets and bedroom sets done in this fashion, and we wistfully dream of having such pieces in our home.

Each piece of wood that has turquoise inlay is unique to the wood and to the spirit of the artist on the day the piece is created. "Let the wood lead the way. There is no right or wrong way to design and create turquoise inlay works of art. Just follow your heart and mind and you will come up with something completely unique and true to your artistic nature," says Jimmy Cook, another inlay artist from Colorado.

No matter the shape or size, I dearly love wood inlaid with turquoise!

A Walk in the Forest

It was a clear winter morning. The sun cast its feeble rays on Mother Earth, as she slumbered below a fresh blanket of snow. The wind murmured quietly through the trees, and a lone wolf announced his presence in the forest.

As I began my walk in the forest, a light flurry of snow began to drift down, the large dry flakes dancing in the breeze. And I was happy.

After a short while, I saw a figure on the trail, waiting patiently for me to approach. My dim, watery eyes thought at first it might be a bear, but then I saw it was an old woman with a bear skin for a coat. She smiled at me as I came closer.

When I came up to her on the trail, she quietly asked me if she could walk with me for a while, and I agreed. We walked silently for a few paces, then she asked me if I could tell her my story. It felt very natural to do so, so I began.

I started by telling her of growing up among the People, of playing with my friends and doing the tasks set by my mother. I told her of learning the dances, and learning more and more of the stories of our People. I told her of the first time that my father, a strong and silent man, took me to hunt for game, and how I cleverly trapped a fat rabbit for our meal. I told her that one day, my mother looked at me and asked me if I was happy. I remember that moment very clearly, as I told my mother that yes, I was indeed happy. She was pleased.

As time went by, I began to notice that one of the girls in our village was watching me from time to time. She had the most beautiful brown eyes, and a perfectly smooth skin the color of a fawn. One day we talked, and my heart pounded like the biggest dance drums. We became friends, and later we decided to join our families with a big wedding feast.

One day, my wonderful wife placed my hand on her growing stomach, and told me that we were going to have a son. She asked me if I was happy, and I told her yes, I was indeed happy. She was pleased.

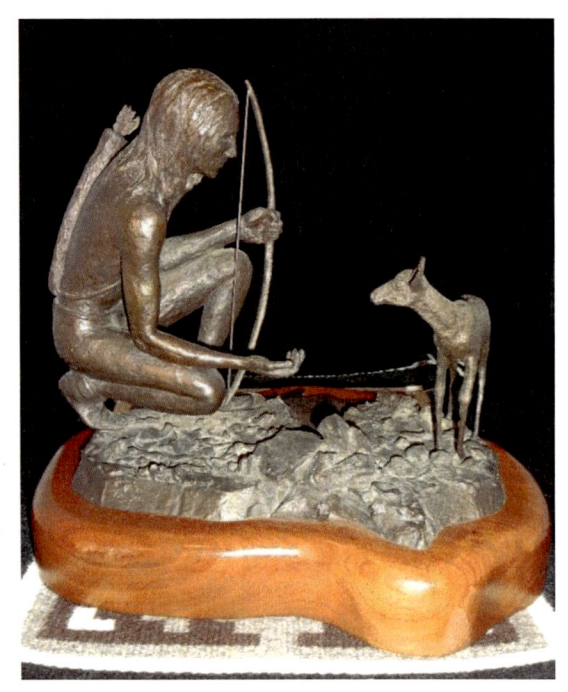

Little Brother, bronze by Bob Bell, Choctaw, circa 1978.

My son grew strong, and he learned the stories and customs of our People. He learned the dances, and he learned from me how to hunt wild game. And one day, he came to me and spoke to me of a certain young girl, who had the most beautiful brown eyes, and a perfectly smooth skin the color of a fawn.

Soon thereafter, we had a wonderful wedding feast, and I danced with the People, as we have done from the beginning of our creation. In a blink of an eye, I watched as my son raised his son, and soon took him on the game trails for his first hunt.

A few winters passed, and my wife and I were settling for our evening sleep. She turned to me and asked me if I still loved her, as her skin was covered in scars and wrinkles from living. I said that of course I still loved her, as she was the most important person in my life. She smiled, and then asked me if I was happy. I told her yes, indeed I was happy. Again, she smiled and was pleased.

The next morning, I awoke, but she was still. Her face had the same smile on it that she always had. I cried, and my family gathered around and tried to comfort me. I began to take long walks in the forest each day, as the peace and harmony of Mother Earth reminded me so much of the gentle soul who had chosen me as her life mate.

I fell silent for a few minutes, as I remembered my love's face, and how tenderly she touched me. My companion on the trail stopped walking, as did I. The snow stopped falling for a bit, and the forest was very still. And then my companion broke the silence with a question. "Are you happy?" she asked. And I replied, "Yes, Mother, indeed I am happy." And she smiled, and was pleased. And my story ended.

Southwest Mountains, original oil painting by J. Barnsley.

Out and about on new adventures...

Made in the USA
San Bernardino, CA
24 August 2016